DIY HYDROPONICS

AND

GROWING MARIJUANA FOR BEGINNERS

BIBLE

2-in-1. The most comprehensive step by step bundle that will show you the best secrets that no one reveals to you about growing marijuana (indoor/outdoor) and hydroponics for a quick growth of your crop.

JHONNY GREEN

advice. The content within this book has been derived from various sources. Please consult a licensed professional before attempting any techniques outlined in this book.

By reading this document, the reader agrees that under no circumstances is the author responsible for any losses, direct or indirect, which are incurred as a result of the use of information contained within this document, including, but not limited to, — errors, omissions, or inaccuracies.

DEDICATION

As a small sign of thanks for buying this book, I would like to offer a free bonus to my readers. To speed up your learning, I want to give you additional tips that I will send you by email. I will also give you answers to your doubts and everything you want to ask me, making you a great expert. Anyway this book will provide you with all the information you need, but I am here for anything.

This is my email: **jhonny_green325@hotmail.com**

TABLE OF CONTENTS

DIY HYDROPONICS

GROWING MARIJUANA FOR BEGINNERS BIBLE

DIY HYDROPONICS

A complete step by step guide for beginners that will show you the techniques to build 6 easy and cost effective hydroponic systems in your house or garden, explaining what the best kept secrets for a fast growth of fruit, vegetable and herbs are.

CHAPTER 1: HISTORY OF HYDROPONICS AND THE SCIENCE BEHIND IT

The word hydroponics was created from its roots which is 'hydro'-water as well as 'ponos'-labor. This type of gardening doesn't need soil. This could seem like something far-reaching and high in technology, but it isn't. Hydroponics is technology inclined whose roots is deeply entrenched on the earth's surface and can be found even in its origin. It can be said to be one of the growing mechanisms that have been in the oldest formation, in the time of simple algae, as well as bacteria that is photosynthetic which were in existence before plants (terrestrial) and all these help the environment to produce the oxygen we breathe in daily. Hydroponics wasn't identified with the name as far back in earlier times where a lot of experiments were carried out to find out the composition of plants but the advent of Modern Hydroponics made things easier.

Examples of such a garden in earlier times which depicted the hydroponics method are the Hanging Gardens of Babylon as well as the Floating Gardens of China. Hydroponics has been used by humans who used these same methods thousands of years back. Technology in modernized times has made it easier to grow plants more rapidly, resilient, as well as in good health. One of Francis Bacon's first works was published on growing terrestrial plants without the use of soil. This is evidenced in the book written by Sylva Sylvarum in the year 1627. Francis Bacon's book 'A Natural History' was published a year after he died. The technique involving the use of water culture became widespread research after. In 1699 John Woodward discovered through the use of water culture that sources of water that were less pure actually grew way better than distilled water infused plants. There was an understanding in 1842 when nine elements were compiled in a list which shows that they are important for plant growth. This came alongside associate discoveries made by botanists of German origin Julius von Sachs and Wilhelm Knop, from 1859 to 1875 and this lead to the discovery and improvement in soilless cultivation development. Solution culture is known to be plants that are terrestrial growing in a soilless form with solutions that have mineral nutrients. It quickly became a standard research and teaching technique and is still widely used. Solution culture is now considered a type of hydroponics where there is an inert medium. In the 1930s, an investigation began by plant scientists on diseases that specific plants have, they observed the symptoms which the plants showed were related to the prevailing soil conditions. Experiments on water culture with this perspective were performed on plants under controlled conditions with the aim of providing symptoms that are similar. In 1929 William Frederick Gericke (1882 – 1970) of the University of California, Berkeley started to promote publicly that in agricultural production of crops, solution culture should be used. William Fredrick Gericke was the earliest reference in modern times in the last hundred years to hydroponics going back in time. He theorized and made popular the ideology that plants while in a solution filled with nutrients alongside water can be grown, when he was in the University of California, Berkley. Unsurprisingly, his colleagues including the public in general had doubts about what he claimed. He had to show them solid proofs of his assumptions by immediately setting out to build a twenty-five-foot-high tomato vine in which he used water as well as nutrients only. He made the decision to call this method of growing plants, 'hydroponics'. The results gotten through the experiments by Gericke were so shocking, it prompted further research into hydroponics as a field. The scientists in University of California carried out further research and amazing benefits were uncovered in relation to cultivation of plants without using soil. Hydroponics is a derivative, coined from the Greek word "υδρωπονικά" (derived from the Greek word "ύδωρ"=water & "πονέω"=cultivate), has analogical construct with γεωπονικά (derived from Greek γαία=earth and πονέω=cultivate), geoponica, concering agriculture, replacing, γεω-, earth, with ύδρο-,

3

water. Frederick Gericke misjudged unfortunately the timing for the introduction of the technical application in general of hydroponics, not knowing it wasn't yet time. Readings of Gericke's report discussed that hydroponics will eventually transform plant agriculture prompted a huge number of requests for further information. Access to the University's greenhouse wasn't given to Gericke by the administration. They were skeptical about his supposed experiments but wanted to coerce him to show them his initial nutrient formulas which he had developed at home. He instead asked to be given access to the space in the greenhouse so that he could improve his nutrient formulas with the appropriate facilities for research. Dennis Robert Hoagland, as well as Daniel Israel Arnon, was given the task by the University to re-evaluate his claims. Hogland's view of Gericke's claims was that the formula he used was of no benefit when compared with plants grown using soil. Gericke's book "Complete Guide to Soilless Gardening" was published in 1940 in an atmosphere that was harsh politically. It was during this time he published for the first time, his basic formula involving the macro- and micronutrient salts for hydroponically-grown plants.

Dennis Robert Hoagland, as well as Daniel Israel Arnon, wrote in the agricultural bulletin printed in 1938 a classic titled," The Water Culture Method for Growing Plants Without Soil" borne out of the research they carried out to refute Gericke's claims. In the book, it was said that crop produced as a result of using hydroponics method is not better in comparison with crop produced from soils that are of good quality. As a result of research of Gericke's claims by order of the University of California, Dennis Robert Hoagland and Daniel Israel Arnon wrote a classic in the 1938 agricultural bulletin, The Water Culture Method for Growing Plants Without Soil, which made the claim that hydroponic crop yields were no better than crop yields with good-quality soils. Eventually, yields from crops would have other factors different from mineral nutrients that could be limiting most especially light. The study they carried out didn't sufficiently appreciate or consider the possibility that hydroponics could have other significant benefits as well as the fact that plant roots have access to oxygen constantly and the plants can have access to water easily no matter how much or how little it may need. This factor is essential due to the fact that overwatering/under watering is one of the most common mistakes when growing a plant; hydroponics averts this when large volumes of water that could make the roots system in the soil drown can be made easily accessible to the plant and if there is an excess of water that isn't needed, it is drained away, aerated actively or recirculated. This helps in the elimination of conditions that could be anoxic. A grower using soil needs to have adequate experience to know the exact amount of water a plant needs. The plant won't be able to have access to oxygen if there is too much water, and if there is too little its ability to have nutrients transported will be lost which characteristically moves while in solution into the roots. The views upheld by Hoagland with assistance from the University which were helpful propelled the two researchers to develop a number of innovative formulas for mineral nutrient solutions that are known universally as *''Hoagland's solution''*. Improved versions of Hoagland solutions are still in use as well as Gericke proposed hydroponic techniques.

In 1930s, at Woke Island, alongside the Pacific Ocean on a rocky atoll, hydroponics was used to grow vegetables for the passengers. This was one of the first successes in the usage of hydroponics. On Woke Island, it was absolutely necessary because it was excessively expensive to airlift in vegetables that are fresh.

Daniel I. Arnon who served in the United States Army as a major (1943 - 1946), used his earlier proficiency in plant nutrition to grow crops in nutrient rich water as well as in gravel since there was no arable land obtainable. The crops were used to feed the troops situated on the barren land of Ponape Island in western Pacific where he served. The Nutrient film technique was developed by Allen Cooper of England in 1982. In the 1960s, the Land Pavilion at Walt Disney World's EPCOT Center was open, and features prominently various hydroponic techniques. Wide-ranging research on hydroponics has been carried out by NASA for its Controlled

Ecological Life Support (CELSS).

For instance, Eurofresh Farms in Willcox, Arizona, in 2007 had more than 200 million pounds of hydroponically grown tomatoes sold. In the area occupied by hydroponic greenhouses commercially, Eurofresh represents one- third of commercially owned greenhouse in the area in the U.S and possesses 318 acres (1.3 km2) under glass. Eurofresh tomatoes were pesticide-free, grown in rockwool with top irrigation. Eurofresh declared bankruptcy, and the greenhouses were acquired by NatureSweet Ltd. in 2013.

There were hundreds acres of commercial hydroponic greenhouses on a large scale that had in production: cucumbers, peppers as well as tomatoes as at 2017.

Over the years, there has been advancement in terms of technology within the industry as well as several economic factors, due to this the global hydroponics market has been forecasted to have a growth rate of US$226.45 million in 2016 to US$724.87 million by 2023.

Let us try to think out of the box. This is a "soilless" scenario. We are all used to seeing plants being grown using soil in fields and gardens that anything will seem absolutely astonishing. But this method is for real. Plants will not only grow without a soil but even grow far better when their roots are immersed in water or air that is very moist. Hydroponics is all about soilless planting. It might seem strange but lots of foods we eat including tomatoes are at present grown hydroponically. Let us look further on how hydroponics works!

What is hydroponics?

Photosynthesis is the process through which plants grow, through the use of sunlight with the chemical present in their leaves knows as chlorophyll that coverts carbon dioxide which is a gas in the air, converts water to glucose (a variety of sugar) and oxygen. This is shown in the chemical equation as seen below (when written out chemically): $6CO_2 + 6H_2O \rightarrow C_6H_{12}O_6 + 6O_2$

Looking at the equation critically, we can see that soil wasn't mentioned at any point. This shows that without soil, plants can actually grow. It is all the proof that is needed that without soil, plants can grow. What is essential for plants is water as well as nutrients which can be gotten from the soil easily. If it is possible that they can access water and nutrients from someplace else-like making their roots stand in solution that is rich in nutrient- then they can do without soil in totality. This is just the simple principle guiding Hydroponics. Theoretically, hydroponics simply means plants grown in water but plants can be grown without it really standing in water so therefore, people mostly prefer to define hydroponics to imply soilless growing of plants. (soilless-without the use of soil). Hydroponics is a subgroup of hydroculture- a technique used for plant growing with no soil, using as an alternative mineral nutrient solution in a water based solvent. Land Plants could grow through making their roots wide open in the mineral nutrient solution or plant roots could be reinforced physically with an inert medium such as gravel, perlite or other substrates. Notwithstanding inert media, changes can be caused by the roots on rhizosphere pH as well as roots exudates which in turn impacts rhizosphere biology. In hydroponic systems, nutrients used in them come from a range of sources that are different. These sources include but are not limited to: duck manure, fish excrement, artificial nutrient solutions, or paid for chemical fertilizers. Usually, plants grown on inert media consists of cucumbers, marijuana, tomatoes, lettuces, pepper as well as model plants such as Arabidopsis thaliana.

Why are things grown hydroponically?

Hydroponics have been challenged several times in terms of how beneficial it could be but there are obviously many advantages to soilless plant growing. Some people that delved into hydroponic method of growing plants experienced more yields that are many times greater than when they used predictable (conventional) methods. Due to the fact that using hydroponics method for planting involves plants being dipped inside nutrient rich solutions directly, a smaller root system is needed so that additional energy can be diverted into the growth of the stem as well as leaf. With roots that are smaller, plants can be grown within the same area and more yields will be gotten (this is good especially when you are growing your plants within a limited area such as a greenhouse, inside a window ledge or a balcony). Amazingly, hydroponic plants do grow faster! Hydroponic method of growing plants helps in the avoidance of pest infestation since you are not using a soil because most of them are carried in the soil. Fewer diseases will be experienced by the plants because the method used is more hygienic. Things are now so much more easily done with the advance in technology such as automated systems which are controlled with timers as well as computers. Everything is not as easy as it seems; there will always be some downsides. First, is the cost of equipment needed such as pumps, containers, nutrients, lights etc. The second downside is seen in the hydroponic-the ponic part of the word (A particular amount of toil is involved). Growing plants using hydroponic method is more scientific because plants are grown in a controlled environment- an environment controlled by you unlike conventional ways of growing plants in which plant growth is determined by the weather, or other conditions, you could be lax sometimes on your treatment of the plants and they will still grow well. Under hydroponics method, you need to constantly keep watch over the plants so they can grow well under the specific conditions needed- such as the use of automated systems for instance lighting timers which makes things quiet easy. The third downside (not much of a downside though) is that because plants have root systems that are similar- smaller, they won't be able to support themselves as well as they should. Plants that have heavy fruiting will need quite a number of intricate types of support.

Photo: Waste not, want not: A researcher at the US Department of Agriculture examines the roots of a hydroponic strawberry plant that's being nourished on wastewater from a trout farm! Photo by Scott Bauer courtesy of <u>US Department of Agriculture (USDA) Agricultural Research Service (ARS)</u>.

How does hydroponics work?

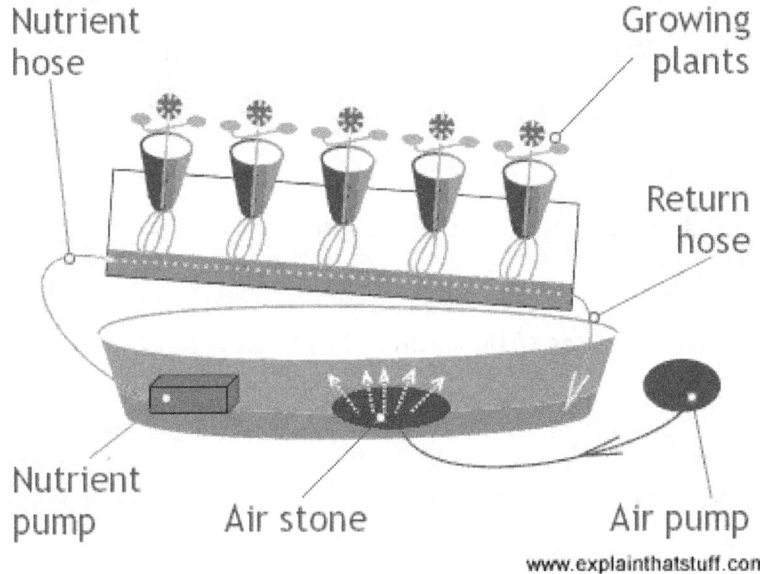

Nutrient hose

Growing plants

Return hose

Nutrient pump

Air stone

Air pump

www.explainthatstuff.com

Artwork: In the nutrient-film technique, nutrient constantly drips past the roots of the plants, which grow out from an inclined tray. The nutrient is pumped back up to the tray and a second pump adds oxygen through an air stone (a piece of porous rock that lets air bubble through it—just like in a fish tank).

When growing plants using hydroponics, there are various ways that can be used. A popular technique is when you let your plants stand in a trough made of plastic and the nutrient infused solution is let to seep gradually past their roots- this is done with the assistance of gravity as well as a pump. This is known as the Nutrient-film technique in which the nutrient emulates a conveyor belt but in liquid form. It is continually slipping past the roots to deliver the rich nutrients they need to grow. This is further explained in CHAPTER TWO. You can alternatively grow your plants with their roots having support from nutrient-rich media such as sand, vermiculite, or Rockwool which serves as a sterile substitute for soil. In theory, hydroponically you can grow any type of plant; but not all plants would thrive well-a similar case with gardening. There are plants that do well such as fruit crops that consists of tomatoes, strawberries, also lettuces as well as herbs.

Hydroponic Vegetables: Are they as Nutritious as those Grown in Soil?

Credit Jason Henry for The New York Times

Are vegetables grown hydroponically as nutritious as those grown in soil?

Vegetables grown hydroponically can be as nutritious as those grown with soil. It is all dependent on the nutrient enriched solution that is used. "In as much as I think that when growing your plants using soil is really great, hydroponics has come a long way," said Marion Nestle, a professor of nutrition, food studies and public health at New York University. He further said, "I have seen producers of hydroponic plants test their vegetables to see if it possesses significant nutrients, and the amount of nutrients fall within the limits that are considered normal for a crop and at times it could even be higher. Conventionally, plants get their nutrients from the soil while hydroponically grown plants get their nutrients from solutions. Hydroponic plants are usually grown in warehouses that are large or greenhouses; they are well-arranged indoors most often on high shelves. They also have a reliance on artificial lighting instead of the natural sunlight. Naturally, vitamins are made by plants, and this means that whether a leafy plant (vegetable) is grown using a soil or soilless (grown hydroponically), the vitamin levels incline towards similarity. What can vary in hydroponic plants is the mineral content which is dependent on the fertilizer that was used. Allen V. Baker who was a professor (Stockbridge School of Agriculture at the University of Massachusetts, Amherst) ascertained that the level of plant's nutrients can be enhanced when you to the solution the plants are being grown in, you simply add nutrients. You can augment the solution with whatever you see fit such as: Calcium-Ca2-, Magnesium- Mg2-, or minor elements like Zinc (Zn2-) or Iron (Fe3-). Allen V. Barker further said that leafy plants (vegetables) grown using hydroponic method could most likely be "superior nutritionally" compared to conventionally grown vegetables.

It should be noted that nutrient content can vary for crops in general, notwithstanding the method used for growing the plants. This difference is in relation to:

• The type of fruit/vegetable.

• When the fruit/vegetable is harvested (time/year).

• The time frame between the harvest period and when the crop is consumed.

• How the crop is handled and the storage process starting from the farm to the fork.

Also, it should be remembered that the nutrient levels differences are not likely to have a substantial influence in general health wise. The most important message given by nutrition experts is the more vegetables eaten, the better for you.

Advantages of using Hydroponics

- There are numerous advantages associated with hydroponics. The greatest is the increasing growth rate of your plant. With hydroponics comes with many advantages, the biggest of which is a greatly increased rate of growth in your plants. With the appropriate structure, your plants will develop faster (at the rate of 25%) and its production rate will increase by 30% more than plants grown using soil.

- Due to the fact that your plant has access to nutrients easily, they don't work hard to get it, and the plants will become larger in size and grow at a fast rate. A root system that is small can even make available exactly what the plant needs. The plants main focus will be on growing up, instead of the expansion of the root system down.

- Through controlling of the nutrient enriched solution as well as pH levels with appropriate care, all the above listed is possible. A Hydroponic system is enclosed; this implies that the system will use lesser water than plants that are grown in soil leading to less evaporation. Whether you believe it or not, if you want to know what is good for the environment, hydroponics is way better due to the fact that it decreases waste as well as pollution that could occur when the soil runs off.

- There are places where the soil isn't suitable enough for planting crops, or they are disease contaminated. Crops can be grown using hydroponics method in such places.

- It eliminates labor needed for cultivation, tilling, fumigation, watering, and various other conventional practices.

- The hydroponic system makes yields are possible on a maximum level, which makes land areas that are expensive and also high in density feasible economically. A feature possessed by all systems is the conservation of water as well as nutrients. This all can lead to reduced pollution of land as well as streams due to the fact that chemicals that are valuable shouldn't be lost.

- Plant diseases gotten through soil can easily be eliminated in closed systems which are flooded in totality with eradicant.

- When using this type of system, you have more complete environmental control, and this is a general feature possessed by the system- root environment, irrigation or well-timed nutrient feeding. And when operating a greenhouse- the light, humidity, temperature, as well as composition of the air can be influenced.

- Water that has high soluble salts in it can be used but it must be done with extreme attention. If the water supply has a soluble salt concentration of over 550 ppm, an open hydroponic system can be used and adequate attention given to the recurrent leaching of the growth medium to enable reduction in the accumulations of salt.

- Hydroponic system can be adopted by an amateur horticulturist for home as well as patio-type gardens, and also in high-rise gardens. A hydroponic system can be clean, lightweight, as well as automated.

- Every single one of the nutrients that are supplied to the plants is available readily.

- The nutrients can be used even when the concentrations are lesser.

- To guarantee optimality in nutrient uptake, the nutrient solution pH can be controlled.

  - Nutrients loss doesn't occur because of leaching.

Disadvantages of Hydroponics

- Notwithstanding the fact that there are numerous advantages that a hydroponics system has, there are some disadvantages. The principal aspect for most people is that hydroponics system of good quality is quiet expensive no matter the size compared with planting with soil. Well, looking at it from another angle, dirt isn't really expensive; you actually get what you have paid for.

- A hydroponics system on a large scale needs a lot of time when setting it up especially if you aren't that experienced as a grower. Additionally, the management of your hydroponics system can also take so much time. There has to be adequate monitoring as well as balancing of your pH and also nutrient levels on a regular basis.

- The hydroponic system utmost threat/risk is that something that seems as simple as a pump failure can potentially -depending on your system size, kills off all your plants within hours. The plants can quickly die due to the fact that the growing medium doesn't stockpile water unlike soil, which implies that the plants have total dependence on the supply of fresh water.

- The original construction cost per acre is huge.

- The rising operation must be directed by trained personnel.

Adequate understanding of how plants grow as well as the principle of nutrition is highly essential.

- If soil induced diseases as well as nematodes are introduced; in a closed system, it may quickly extend to all the beds on similar nutrient tank.

- Almost all existing varieties of plants that have been modified to a growing environment that is controlled will need research and development.

- Plant's react to a nutrition that is either good or poor in a way that is incredibly fast. Plants must be observed everyday by the grower.

  - If there is any decline in the oxygen tension of the nutrient solution; this can generate a situation that is anoxic and leads to an inhibition of ion uptake.

Elemental Compound and Ion Symbol Designation

In this textbook, all the elements are selected by their symbols. The symbols for those elements, compounds, and ions found in this text are as follows:

Element	Symbol	Element	Symbol
Aluminum	Al	Nickel	Ni
Antimony	Sb	Nitrogen	N
Arsenic	As	Oxygen	O
Boron	B	Phosphorus	P
Bromine	Br	Platinum	Pt
Cadmium	Cd	Potassium	K
Chlorine	Cl	Rubidium	Rb
Chromium	Cr	Selenium	Se

Cobalt	Co	Silicon	Si
Copper	Cu	Silver	Ag
Fluoride	F	Sodium	Na
Indium	In	Strontium	Sr
Iodine	I	Sulfur	S
Iron	Fe	Titanium	Ti
Lead	Pb	Uranium	U
Lithium	Li	Vanadium	V
Magnesium	Mg	Yttrium	Y
Manganese	Mn	Zinc	Zn
Molybdenum	Mo		

Compound/ Ion	Symbol
Acetate	$C_2H_3O_2$
Ammonium	NH_4^+
Arsenate	AsO_4^{2-}
Bicarbonate	HCO_3
Borate	BO_3^{3-}

Carbon dioxide	CO_3^{2-}
Carbonate	CO_3^{2-}
Cyanide	CN^-
Dihydrogen phosphate	$H_2PO_4^-$
Monohydrogen phosphate	HPO_4^{2-}
Nitrate	NO_3^-
Nitrite	NO_2^-
Phosphate (ortho)	PO_4^{3-}
Silicate	SiO_4
Sulfate	SO_4^{2-}
Water	H_2O

CHAPTER 2: THE TYPES OF HYDROPONIC SYSTEMS

Hydroponic system is so amazing; it has several different types that are available. There are some hydroponic systems that are among the best available in the market that is a combination of different kinds of hydroponics merged into a singular hydroponic system which is known as an HYBRID. Hydroponics is so distinct; it has numerous techniques that you can use to access the nutrient enriched solution for your plants. The different types of hydroponic systems are:

1. **Deepwater Culture**

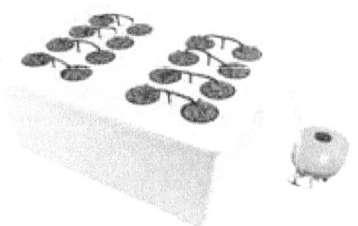

Deepwater Culture (DWC), known also as "reservoir method", and is the easiest technique so far when it comes to plants growth using hydroponics. In a DWC hydroponic system, the roots are suspended in a nutrient enriched solution. The nutrient enriched solution is oxygenated by an aquarium air pump-this assist in preventing the plant roots from drowning.

NOTE: Avoid light from penetrating your system-it can trigger algae growth. This could cause boundless devastation to your system.

The key benefit when using the Deepwater Culture System is that clogging of drip or spray emitters is non-existent. It makes Deep Water Culture a first-rate choice for organic hydroponics-hydroponics system that makes use of organic nutrients are disposed to having clogs.

The *deep water culture* technique being used to produce _"Hungarian wax peppers"_ Conventional method using deep water culture technique prefers the use of buckets that are made of plastic as well as large containers. The plant is confined in a net pot that is suspended from the lid's centre while the suspended in the nutrient enriched solution are the roots. The air pump saturates the solution with oxygen which is in combination with porous stones. Using deep water culture technique makes the plants grow faster due to the high volume of oxygen the roots obtain. The Kratky Method has similarity to the DWC, the only difference is that it uses non-circulating water reservoir.

2. Nutrient Film Technique

Nutrient Film Technique (NFT) is a kind of hydroponic system in which there is a continuous flow of nutrient enriched solution that flows over the plants roots. The design is very simple yet so operational and widely popular among the growers of plant using hydroponic methods. This solution type flows with the force of gravity because it is on a slight tilt.

This kind of hydroponic system works perfectly well due to the fact that the plant roots have more oxygen absorbed from the air than from the nutrient solution itself. The plant gets oxygen easily since it is only the root tips that have contact with the nutrient enriched solution. This aids the plant to have a grow rate that is quiet fast.

Nutrient Film Technique use the components that are similar to that of Ebb & Flow Technique. There is similarity between them in that they use similarly water pumps for the delivery of nutrients to your crops. The different is in their individual configuration. The difference is that Ebb & Flow uses the mechanics of Flood and Drain but for NFT, it uses the mechanics of the system flowing in a constant way. There are other systems such as Wicking and also Kratky Method but they do not make the provision of optimum conditions for the crops even though they are passive, very simple to build as well as easy to use. Nutrient Film Technique is usually used for growing plants that are smaller in size yet fast in growth. For instance, variety of lettuces can be grown using the Nutrient Film Technique. Other from lettuces, commercialized growers make use of the Nutrient Film Technique to grow various herbs, baby greens as well as strawberries. Also with NFT you can grow variety of leaves such as Bibb as well as Cos Type (Romaine), lettuces, kales, mustard greens as well as many oriental vegetables including herbs.

Also you can plant flowers that are edible and can be added to make salad very rich and make presentation of food to look sensational. Examples of such flowers that are edible are; nasturtiums as well as pansies.

NFT system can also be used to get responses that are fast, then new seedlings can then be planted for future harvesting. This will make the dream of any home hobbyist to be fulfilled because he/she has a garden and there is continual supply of crops.

3. Aeroponics

Aeroponics is another hydroponics technique in which the plant roots when being suspended in the air, are mist up with a nutrient enriched solution. These are done with devices for misting that are specially made. Plants are nurtured basically with nothing but mist laden with nutrient. This hydroponic system technique as a concept is where the plant roots are held in a medium that is soilless in nature. The growing medium such as coco-noir; where intermittently the water livened with nutrient is pumped. In Aeroponics, the seeds get embedded in the bits of foam that are squeezed into tiny pots. They are exposed to light at one end and misted nutrient spray at the other end. Also holding the stem in place as well as the root mass is the foam as the plants grow. There are two main processes that can be used to get the nutrient solution on the roots that are exposed. The first process mists the roots by using a fine spray nozzle while the second process uses a ''pond fogger''. If you make the decision of selecting the process of using a pond fogger, you have to ensure the usage of a Teflon coated disc-this will assist in reduction on the extent of maintenance needed. Who would ever think that naked roots can actually thrive and have a survival trait. It has been discovered that when the growing medium is removed from the equation it makes the plants root to be very free. They are exposed to oxygen; and this hastens and leads to more rapid growth. Aeroponics is widely used because it is tremendously efficient in terms of water. It uses less water. It is a closed system that is looped and uses ninety-five percent lesser irrigation compared to traditional farming of using soil to grow plants. The nutrients that are also held in the water gets recycled too. It has the capability of large numbers of crops to be grown in a small space. Due to the fact that the crops are grown in spaces that are enclosed, the nutrient does not run off to adjacent waterways. Although, Aeroponics is technical because it needed power to make the mist system work. For instance, AeroGarden, which is a commercialized aeroponics system makes it an exceptional entry point to using aeroponics technique. It needs just a little setting up because it is a turn-key system. It has good support as well as supplies that can give you the needed start up push.

4. Wicking

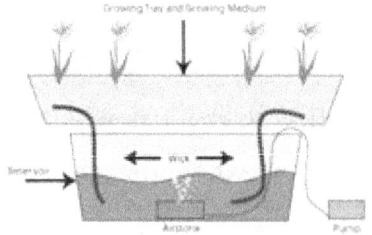

Wicking is a hydroponic technique that is easy to use and has the lowermost costing. They are the utmost uncomplicated system of hydroponics. It is also as a good introduction for students that want to understand the basics of hydroponics without delving into the uncomplicated parts of the other systems.

Wick systems are passively active; this means generally that they possess no part that moves. It makes them cheap as well as easy to maintain than other systems such as Ebb and Flow. Although they cannot be use for plants that need higher upkeep. Or even plants that are large, and ingest loads of water. The idea that brings forth wicking is when you have a material, for instance cotton, surrounded by a growing medium in which an end of the wick material is positioned in the nutrient enriched solution. The solution is at that juncture wicked to the plants roots. This kind of hydroponic system can be made simpler by the removal of the wick material totally and substituting it with a medium which possesses the capability to wick nutrients to the plants roots. How does this work? It works through the suspension of your medium's bottom right in the solution. Medium that are recommended for use are; perlite or vermiculite. Mediums to be avoided include; coconut coir, Rockwool, or peat moss- they may absorb your nutrient solution greatly which may end up suffocating the plant.

5. Passive sub-irrigation

**Water plant**-**cultivated** **crocus** Passive sub-irrigation, also known as passive hydroponics, semi-hydroponics, or _hydroculture_, is a technique in which growing of plants in a porous medium that is inert which aids in the transportation of water as well as fertilizer to the plant roots through capillary action from a separate reservoir as required. This reduces labor as well as provides a steady supply of water to the plant roots. In a simple way, in a shallow solution of fertilizer as well as water sits a pot or it could be on a capillary mat that is saturated with nutrient enriched solutions.   There   are various medium available for usage such as coconut husk as well as

expanded   clay   that   comprises   of   enough   air   spaces   than   the traditional potting mixes, increased oxygen is delivered to the plant roots and this is necessary in epiphytic plants –like orchids as well as bromeliads, whose roots are naturally exposed to air. Extra benefits of using passive hydroponics system are that it reduces root rot as well as the surplus ambient humidity it provides through evaporations.

When comparing passive sub-irrigation to traditional ways of farming in terms of crop per yield fares better because:

- ☐ It uses thirteen times lesser water in a crop cycle unlike traditional system of farming

- ☐ It uses on an average hundred times more energy (kilojoules per kilogram) than traditional system of farming.

6. Drip System

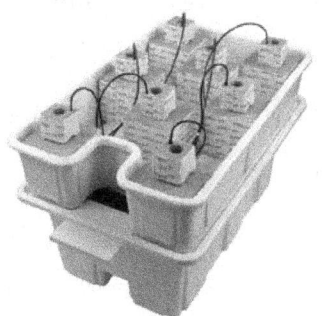

Another type of hydroponics is the drip system which is rather simple. This system is very popular and borrows from the utmost proficient water- irrigation system that is used in cultivating plants traditionally. It is being used to produce crops that are bountiful by every person from the people dwelling in the city to those living in apartments that are small, to some of the largest hydroponic farms that are commercialized and working on a large scale globally. How does the drip system work? It works through the sluggish feed of does the drip system work? It works through the sluggish feed of nutrient enriched solution to the hydroponics medium. Recommended are slow draining medium such as coconut coir,

rockwool or peat moss. You can also use medium that are fast draining even though you would have to use a dripping emitter that is faster.

The drawback of this system is that it is well-known for clogging is the dripper/emitters. It is a system that we prefer not to use, even though it is an effective technique for plant growing if the clogs that affect this system type can be avoided. of a feed of nutrient enriched solution to the hydroponics medium. A drip system works by providing a slow feed of nutrient solution to the hydroponics medium. We recommend using a slow draining medium, such as Rockwool, coconut coir, or peat moss. You can also use a faster draining medium, although you will have to use a faster dripping emitter.

The downside to a system like this is that the drippers / emitter are famous for clogging. We prefer not to use drip systems, but it can be an effective method for growing if you can avoid the clogs that plague this type of system. The reason the system gets clogged is because particles from nutrients that build up in the emitter. Systems that use organic nutrients are more likely to have this kind of issue.

There are two kinds of drip hydroponics system. We have the recovery as well as the non-recovery drip systems.

In a recovery system, recovery happens to the nutrient solution and then it is recycled through the system a multiple of times. In a non-recovery system, it is actually more efficient resource wise and hence the preferred technique used by commercial hydroponic plant growers. In this type of system, the nutrient solution is not recycled, Herein, you just need to make sure your nutrient reservoir is refilled regularly.

7. Top-fed deep water culture

Top-fed deep water culture is a technique that involves the delivery of extremely oxygenated nutrient solution to zone of the plant roots. Unlike deep water culture technique that involves the roots of the plants to hang downwards into a nutrient solution reservoir, top-fed deep water culture involves pumping of the solution upwards to the plant roots (top-feeding). In a continuously re-circulating system, water is let loose over the roots of the plants and it then runs back to the reservoir underneath. Similarly, with deep water culture, the reservoir has air been pumped into the water via the airstone through a hose that is located at the reservoir's exterior (outside it). The function of the airstone is to assist in the addition of oxygen to the water in use. The airstone as well as the water pump equally work throughout the day. (24 hours per day).

The greatest benefit that top-fed water culture has over the typical deep water culture is growth that increases for the duration of the first few weeks. In deep water culture, the plant roots wouldn't have gotten to the water yet at a point in time; while in top-fed water culture, easily accessible is the water for the plant roots from the very start and they will grow towards the reservoir beneath faster than when you are using a deep water culture system. But once the plants roots have gotten to the reservoir beneath it, the difference between top-fed deep water culture over the typical (standard) deep water culture is negligible. There is no great benefit at this stage. Nonetheless, because the growth is faster at the beginning for the top-fed deep water culture technique, there can be a decrease in growth time by few weeks.

8. Rotary

A rotary hydroponic cultivation demonstration at the Belgian Pavilion Expo in 2015.

A rotary hydroponic garden is a style of commercial hydroponics created within a circular frame which rotates continuously during the entire growth cycle of whatever plant is being grown.

While system specifics vary, systems typically rotate once per hour, giving a plant 24 full turns within the circle each 24-hour period. Within the center of each rotary hydroponic garden can be a high intensity grow light, designed to simulate sunlight, often with the assistance of a mechanized timer.

Each day, as the plants rotate, they are periodically watered with a hydroponic growth solution to provide all nutrients necessary for robust growth. Due to the plants continuous fight against gravity, plants typically mature much more quickly than when grown in soil or other traditional hydroponic growing systems. Due to the small foot print a rotary hydroponic system has, it allows for more plant material to be grown per square foot of floor space than other traditional hydroponic systems.

☐ Ebb and flow (flood and drain) sub-irrigation

☐   (b)

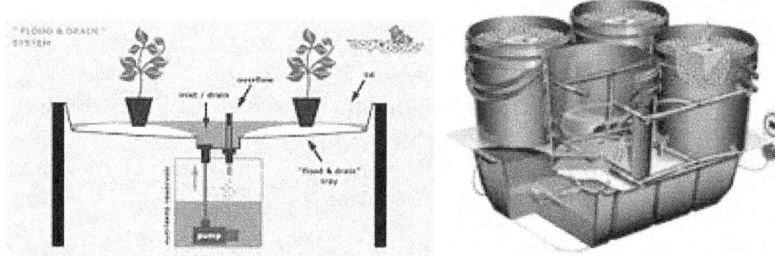

An *ebb and flow*, or *flood and drain*, hydroponics system

The hydroponics system known as ebb and flow, also called flood & drain system, is great for growing plants. This form of hydroponic system works by engulfing the area that is growing with the nutrient solution at particular intervals. Slowly the nutrient solution is drained back into the reservoir. The pump is connected to a timer; this makes the process continually reoccur repeatedly at precise intervals which allows your plants to have access to the volume of nutrients needed.

This type of system is desirable for plants that are used to having spells of dryness. There are particular species of plants that thrive when they have occasional period of dryness which makes their roots to enlarge in their search for moisture. This makes the plant to grow at a faster rate because more nutrients can be absorbed by it.

In its most simple form, there is a tray placed above the reservoir containing the nutrient solution. The tray is filled either with growing medium-most popular being clay granules and directly plant or pot can be positioned over a medium stand inside the tray.

During intervals that are frequent, a timer in its simplicity makes the pump to get filled with nutrient solution, the upper tray. When this is done, the solution gets drained back downwards into the reservoir. The medium through this means is kept frequently flushed with air as well as nutrients. When the upper tray is filled beyond the drain stoppage, it starts to recirculate the water till it gets turned off by the timer. In turn, draining back into the reservoir is the water that has filled up the water tray.

⬚ 9. Run-to-waste

This is another type of hydroponic system. In this type of system, applied periodically to the surface of the medium is the nutrient solution as well as water solution. In 1946, this technique was developed in Bengal, this is why it is often times called "The Bengal System".

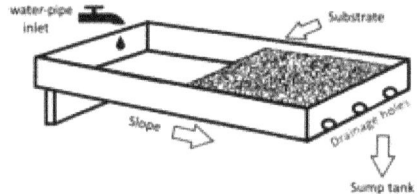

A *run-to-waste* hydroponics system, referred to as "The Bengal System" after the region in eastern India where it was invented (circa 1946).

This technique can be configured in a variety of ways. When it is in its most simple form, a nutrient as well as a water solution is applied manually once or more than one time each day to a container that has inert growing media such as perlite, vermiculite, rockwool, coco fibre or sand. In a system that is a bit more complex, the delivery pump is automatic, with a timer, as well as irrigation tubing which takes delivery of nutrient solution with a frequency governed by the main parameters which are size of the plant, growing stage of the plant, substrate as well as substrate conductivity, climate, ph as well as water content.

In commercial hydroponics, the frequency of watering is having multiple factors and ruled by computers or the PLCs.

The production of big plants such as cucumber, tomatoes, as well as pepper uses a form or another of the run-to-waste hydroponics.

When it comes to protective the environment responsibly, the waste rich in nutrient is gotten and passes through an on the site filtration processing which can be used severally, thereby making very productive, the system.

For instance, there are substrates that are soil-free in which some bonsai grow on. They consist normally of grit, akadama, diatomaceous earth as well as additional inorganic components and delivered in run-to-waste system their water as well as nutrients solution.

☐ 10. Fogponics

Fogponics is a technique used in hydroponics system. It is derived from aeroponics in which there is aerosolizing of the nutrient solution via the diaphragm that vibrate at ultrasonic frequency(ies). This technique produces solution droplets that have the tendency to have a diameter of 5–10 µm, which is smaller than the ones made through forcing a nutrient solution through nozzles that are pressurized as seen in aeroponics. The size of the droplets which is smaller makes them to easily diffuse easily through the air, while delivering to the roots, nutrients wherein access to oxygen is limitless.

Useful Tips

- ☐ It is highly recommended that nutrient solution located in your reservoir should be changed every 2-3 weeks.
- ☐ The temperature of the water in your reservoir should be

kept between 65 & 75 degrees. The water temperature can be maintained by the use of a water heater/water chiller.

- A flexible tubing connected to an air pump with an air stone can assist in increasing circulation as well as keeping oxygenated the nutrient solution.

- When your plant starts to look unhealthy- showing signs of discoloration or distortion; you should check first the ph and adjust it. If it is now seen that the problem isn't the ph level, then you can flush your system using a solution- for instance, Clearex.

- It is highly recommended that the feeding cycle given by the producer of your nutrients should be followed.

- After a growing cycle has ended, you should flush, clean as well as sterilize the entire system. You should have your reservoir drained, all debris removed, and let all your entire system run for like a day with a mixture of non-chlorine bleach as well as water. $1/8^{th}$ of a cup of non-chlorine bleach should be used for each gallon of water. Now, get your system drained and also get it flushed meticulously using clean water so as to do away with any extra bleach remaining.

Why Should Hydroponics Be Chosen?

Hydroponics is an outstanding choice for all categories of growers. It is an outstanding choice because it gives you the capability to accurately control the variables that will affect how healthy your plants will grow. A hydroponic system that is fine-tuned can exceed easily a soil-based system in the quality as well as quantity (amount of crop yield) of the plant. Hydroponics is the best choice for you if you desire to grow the largest, sensational, delicious plants you can possibly imagine. At first, it may seem daunting, especially with all the equipment as well as labor that is involved. But once you can understand the basics, it will become seemingly so simple. You can start small, keep it all simple, and your hydroponic system will be amazing, you will never cease to be stunned.

Are vegetables grown hydroponically as nutritious as those grown in soil?

The bottom line is it depends on the nutrient solution the vegetables are grown in, but hydroponically grown vegetables can be just as nutritious as those grown in soil.

"Much as I think that soil is just great for growing plants, hydroponics has come a long way," said Marion Nestle, a professor of nutrition, food studies and public health at New York University. "I've seen hydroponic producers who have tested their leafy greens for key nutrients, and the amounts fall well within normal limits for their crop and are sometimes even higher."

Traditionally, plants obtain nutrients from soil. With hydroponics, the plants get nutrients from a solution instead. (Aeroponics, in which the plants' roots are suspended in the air, is similar except fertilizer is misted onto the roots.) Usually inhabiting large warehouses or greenhouses, hydroponic plants are arranged indoors, often in tall shelves, and they rely on artificial light rather than sunlight.

Plants make their own vitamins, so vitamin levels tend to be similar whether a vegetable is grown hydroponically or in soil. It's the mineral content that can vary in hydroponic crops, depending on the fertilizer used.

"You can enhance" a plant's nutrient levels "simply by adding nutrients to the solution" they're grown in, said Allen V. Barker, a professor at the Stockbridge School of Agriculture at the University of Massachusetts, Amherst. "You could add whatever you wanted: calcium or magnesium, or minor elements like zinc or iron." The result is that vegetables grown hydroponically could even be "nutritionally superior" to traditionally grown ones, he said.

Keep in mind that nutrient content varies for produce in general, regardless of the growing method. The differences relate to the type of fruit or vegetable, the time of year it is harvested, how long after harvesting the crop gets eaten, and how it is handled and stored from farm to fork.

Remember, too, that these differences in nutrient levels are unlikely to have a significant impact on overall health. The key message from most nutrition experts is simply the more vegetables you eat, the better.

CHAPTER 3: HYDROPHONICS AS A DO IT YOURSELF BUSINESS

Hydroponic System Only Need a Few Basic Parts to Build

☐ **Growing Chamber (or Tray)**

A part of the hydroponic system is the "growing chamber" where the roots of the plants will be growing. To make it simple, the growing chamber is the vessel for the root area. Plant support is provided by this area, and this is also where the roots can have access to the nutrient solution. The roots are also protected from heat, light as well as pests. It is highly important for the root area to be kept cool as well as light proof. The roots can be damaged by light that is prolonged, high temperatures in the root area can lead to heat stress on your plants and fruits as well as flower drop are part of the effect of heat stress. The size as well as shape of the growing chamber is dependent on the kind of hydroponic system in use in your greenhouse building and also the kind of plants that will

be grown in it. Plants that are big in size have root systems that are also big, more space will be needed to hold the plants adequately. There are so many designs that are unending. You can use practically anything as the growing chamber but you should not use anything made out of metal; it could end up corroding or reacting with the nutrients. Many ideas can be gotten, if you look all around you. There are a lot of different materials which can be accessed easily that can be used to build a growing chamber for your hydroponic system.

Reservoir

The reservoir is the also a portion of the hydroponic system which has the nutrient solution in its hold. The nutrient solution comprises of plant nutrients that are mixed in water. You can pump the nutrient solution from the reservoir upwards to the growing chamber (root area), in cycles while using a timer, and it could also be done continuously without the use of a timer; or the roots could even hang downwards into the reservoir 24/7 which makes the reservoir to also be the growing chamber.

The reservoir can be made out of any plastic that could hold water. As far as the plastic does not leak, sufficient water is held by, and it is cleaned very well, it can then be used as a reservoir. A reservoir should be light-proof. If you hold the plastic over your head and light comes through, then it is not light proof. But you can easily make it light proof by putting a cover on it, painting it or you could wrap a bubble wrap installation round it. If the plastic is not light proof, even with levels of low light, algae as well as microorganisms will begin to grow.

Submersible Pump

Almost all hydroponic systems use a submersible pump to pump the nutrient solution (water) from the reservoir upwards to the plant's growing chamber. They can be found easily at any hydroponic supply shop or home improvement stores with garden supplies as fountain and/or Pond pumps. They come in various sizes. Submersible pumps are fundamentally not anything more than an impeller that makes use of an electromagnet to spin it. Submersible pumps can be taken apart easily and then methodically cleaned. If it does not have a filter, one can be made easily by cutting out a piece of furnace filter screen or any material similar to it that would fit. Pump as well as filter should be cleaned on a regular basis.

Delivery System

The delivery system is another part of the hydroponic system. It is a very simple system, exceedingly customizable especially when you are building your own hydroponic system. Apart from the pump, it is simply the system the water or nutrient solution goes through so as to get to the plants roots in the growing chamber and again back towards the reservoir. Normally, the quality as well as simplest materials that can be used for the nutrient/water solution delivery system is to combine the standard PVC tubing and the connectors, standard garden irrigation tubing as well as connectors, and also blue or black vinyl tubing.

Dependent on the kind of hydroponic system you decide to build, you may want to use drip emitters/sprayers as part of the nutrient solution delivery system. Even though they are useful, they can get clogged. You must have additional emitters/ sprayers so you can change it immediately while cleaning out the ones you removed. Most times it is preferable if you can avoid using emitters/sprayers because of it easily clogs and costs additional money as well.

Simple Timer

The kind of hydroponic system been built by you as well as where you place the system to grow will determine the number of timers you may need. It may be one or two. If artificial lighting is used by you instead of natural lighting (sunlight), you may need a timer to control the timing to off as well as on the lighting system. For ebb and flow, drip, and aeroponic systems timer may be required to control the on as well as off times for the submersible water pump. Specific types of aeroponics may require a special timer.

There are standard light times for every day that works perfectly fine for equally the lights and also submersible pumps. It is recommended that the timer should be rated for 15 amps instead of 10 amps. Timers rated 15amps are most times known as heavy duty. Just check the back of the timer or its package for the 15-amp rating. Do try and get a timer for outdoor usage, it usually has a cover and it is customarily water resistant. It is not recommended to use costly digital timers over the analogue dial kind of timer. This is because digital timers when they lose power or are unplugged lose all memory and also all the settings you inputted will be lost even if it all happens within 1s. (with the exception of buying a timer that has a backup battery). They most times do not have a different off as well as off settings in comparison to the analogue kind of timer. Do ensure that the timer gotten has loads of pins all around the dial.

Air Pump

Unlike other equipment needed for the hydroponic system, air pumps are actually optional. They are only needed in the water culture systems. Though their usage has a whole lot of benefits, as well as the fact that they are somewhat cheap. You can find air pumps at any location where aquarium supplies are sold. Air pumps basically just supply air as well as oxygen to the roots as well as water. Pumped via an airline is air leading to the air stones which create a horde of small bubbles that rise up through the nutrient solution. The air pump in a water culture system prevents the plant roots when submerged in the nutrient solution from suffocating 24/7. In any other kind of hydroponic system, the air pump is used usually in the reservoir. It assists in increasing the level of dissolved oxygen in the water as well as keeping the water oxygenated. Other benefits of air pumps usage is that as the air bubbles escalate and rise, it keeps the water as well as nutrients moving and also circulating. This helps the nutrients in remaining evenly mixed always at every time. The circulating oxygenated water assists also

in the reduction of pathogens from achieving a footing in the reservoir.

Growlights

Growlights are part of the hydroponic system that is optional. It is dependent on where you are planning to put your hydroponic system, and also grow your plants. Natural sunlight or artificial light can be chosen by you. You get to decide which you would like to grow your plant with. Natural sunlight is most preferred because it is not expensive and it is basically free. It doesn't even need any additional equipment. Nevertheless, if the location where your plants are does not have enough natural sunlight getting to it, then there will be a definite need for artificial light to grow your plant with. Grow light are dissimilar from the normal household lights. The grow lights are fashioned to radiate definite color spectrums that mimic how the natural sunlight works. These color spectrums (wavelength) are used by plants to conduct photosynthesis. Plants require the conducting of photosynthesis so they can grow, flourish, produce fruits as well as flowers. This shows that the type and also

 amount of light a plant can get will have an effect on its ability to perform photosynthesis as well as grow well.

A huge garden is not needed if you want to grow fresh crops. You do not even need years of experience to start building your ''Do it yourself' (DIY)'' indoor grow system. This is the beauty and what makes hydroponics distinct.

Hydroponics as a whole is based on flexibility as well as inventiveness. We have here 16 selection of the best homemade hydroponic plans that anyone can build. These hydroponic plans comprise of the beginner, intermediate, and expert level setups. They are:

- The Passive Bucket Kratky Method

- Simple Bucket Hydroponic System

- Simple Drip System with Buckets

- Aquarium Hydroponics Raft

- PVC NFT Hydroponics System

- Hydroponic Grow Box

- Frame Hydroponic System

- Vertical Window Farm

- Hydroponic Rain Tower Garden

- Simple Desktop Hydroponic System

- Mason Jar Kratky Method Hydroponics

- Dutch Bucket Hydroponics

- Deep Water Culture Hydroponics

- Drip Water Hydroponics

☐ Ebb-Flow System

☐ Stackable Hydroponics

☐ *The Passive Bucket Kratky*

  Method

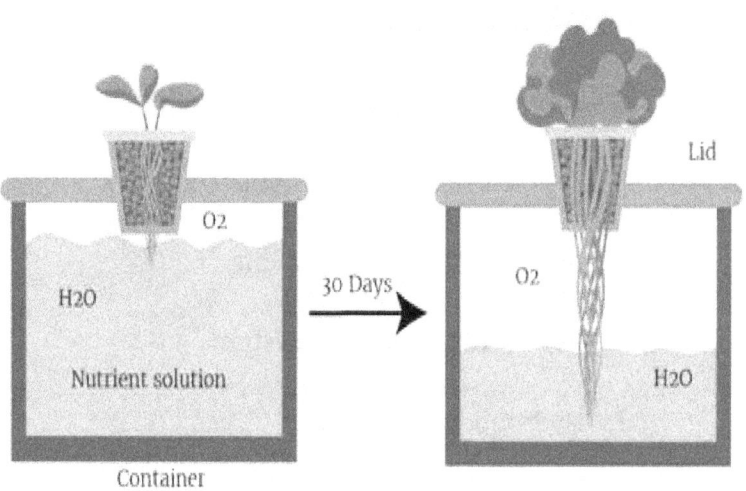

The Kratky Method is with no iota of doubt one of the easiest hydroponic plans that as beginner you can start on your own within quiet a number of hours.

This method is great for anyone who just wants to start up with hydroponics. What you need is a bucket, some growing media (like hydroton, perlite), some net pots, hydroponic nutrients, and pH kits.

These are all required to set up a passive system (no electricity required) that can run automatically for weeks without maintenance.

At the beginning, you can grow green vegetables such as lettuces, spinaches or fruits plants such as tomatoes after you have gotten sufficient experiences. You can try building this system.

[?] **Simple Bucket Hydroponic System**

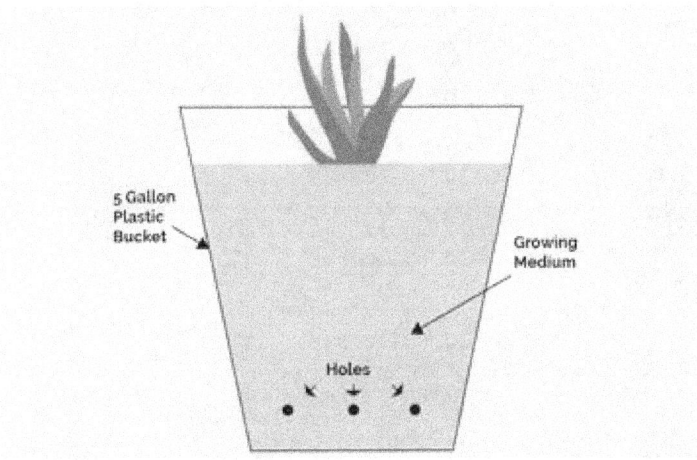

This is another simple hydroponic arrangement for beginners. All that is needed by you is a 5-gallon bucket, some growing media like coco coir or perlite-vermiculite, as well as nutrient mix.

The setup works by using the growing media to make a capillary action, which moves nutrients up to the plants roots.

This system is ideal for single large plants. If you want to keep things basic, you can water the system manually.

For an automated system, you will need another bucket for the reservoir, and a submersible pump, and timer. You can try building this system.

❓ **Simple Drip System with Buckets**

Another entry-level option, this is a bit more advanced than the single bucket system above. It can still be cobbled together using parts that cost less $100 in total.

The original plan calls for growing four plants in separate buckets, all fed by a common reservoir. This is a very flexible setup that can be expanded in Future.

You can change the size of the containers, and reservoir depending on the size of plants involved. You can use large 4-gallon buckets or smaller containers.

Remember to buy a larger reservoir in case you want to add more plants to the mix later on. You can try building this system.

⁈ Aquarium Hydroponics Raft

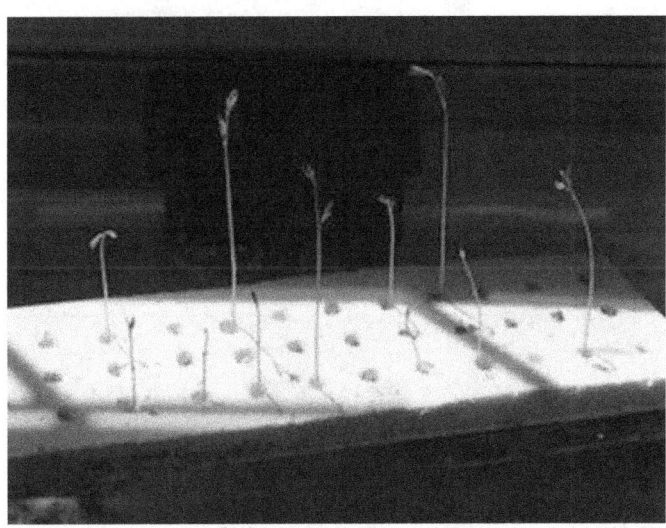

This is a very cool project to get your feet wet in the world of hydroponics. It is also a great way to get your kids hooked to the field.

As the name suggests, you will need an aquarium fish tank to make this work. This system can be used to grow small beans or even a single large lettuce.

Along with the usual ingredients like nutrients, water, and plants, you will need a raft of barge fashioned out of foam. The system can be passive or active, using pumps and electricity. You can try building this system.

- **PVC NFT Hydroponics System**

What is needed to create a Nutrient Film Technique?

- A reservoir that will have in it the appropriate Nutrient Solution

- ☐ A Nutrient Pump

- ☐ Tubes that will distribute water from the Nutrient Pump to the NFT tubes for growing.

- ☐ The appropriate channel needed for the plants growing

- ☐ There should be net pots that can contain plants as well as the growing medium(a) to start planting seedlings with.

- ☐ A system that can return i.e. a tubing channel which can guide the nutrient solution that has been used back to the reservoir.

Large 4 inch PVC pipes can be used to create your homemade hydroponics system. In this plan, the plants are placed in cups which are arranged in holders drilled into the pipes. The system is watered using a reservoir and pump. This is a closed system, with the water circulating between the pipes and the reservoir.

Using the NFT system, it has two components that are important. They are the: grow tray (channel) as well as the reservoir that will contain the water as well as the nutrients.

The grow tray has inside a net pot which also contains the growing medium (a) –perlite, coconut noir, Rockwool. Though in reality, in the NFT system, a lot of growers do not use growing media because the roots have enough moisture, nutrients, as well as oxygen, all gotten from the system.

This works how? When the grow tray is positioned at an angle in which it has the support of the; rack/bench; and then water flows downwards in the direction of the nutrient pipe for returning. Flowing out of this particular pipe will be the extra nutrient solution that is in excess will drift out of the pipe and then there will be movement to the next channel/ tube. At this point, recirculation occurs through the system as a whole.

The plant roots hang downwards to the channel' bottom where they have contact with the film of the nutrient solution that is shallow and then there is an absorbent of the required nutrients from them. The film of the nutrient solution gives the plant a chance to be watered but this does not mean they will be soaked in entirety. The thinness of the nutrient solution gives the upper root the chance to have entrance to oxygen in the air.

 This plan is ideal for growing a lot of small plants within a small area. The basic system can house anywhere from 20-40 plants.

This system can be placed indoors or outdoors. If indoors, grow lights are of course essential.

The hydroponics method used in this plant is called NFT. It is an excellent plan for growing plants like tomatoes. You can try building this system.

⟨?⟩ Hydroponic Grow Box

This DIY plan is a very flexible system that can be moved around quite a lot. It can be made with any sized storage tub or bin. It should have a lid.

The system uses PVC pipes, a submersible pump, and irrigation sprinkler heads to deliver nutrients and water to the plants.

The plants are housed in net cups filled with some growing medium. The lid of the box will house these net cups. This system is on intermediate level. You can try building this system.

⍰ Frame Hydroponic System

The frame hydroponic plan is very similar to the PVC hydroponic system. It uses the same NFT-based principles to feed nutrients and water to the plants.

The difference here is the increased verticality. By adding new layers of PVC pipes at different heights, you can grow more plants in the same space. The amount of tubing required will increase, as will the complexity of the pumping system.

This particular plan houses the PVC pipes on a wooden rack frame. You can grow herbs and plants like strawberries and tomatoes with this system. This is an advanced system. You can try building this system.

⍰ Vertical Window Farm

A unique concept that solves the problem of lighting while also creating a fascinating window display for the outside world.

The plan involves using containers to hold plants in a vertical rack setup. Recycled water bottles make perfect containers.

A system of pipes/tubes to bring nutrients from the reservoir to the plants. Lighting is of course provided by natural sunlight. This plan is ideal for herbs, kale, strawberries, and chard. You can try building this system.

❓ Hydroponic Rain Tower Garden

This is another vertical hydroponics plan that uses a tower-like structure. The entire setup can be created for around $500.

The tower is created using a fence post. The plan can be adapted for indoor and outdoor grows.

The plants are housed in net cups that are spaced evenly across the length of the post in recesses cut into the post.

A pump is used to pump water to the of the tower. The water flows down the inside, reaching every plant from top to bottom. This system is on intermediate level. You can try building this system.

⁇ Simple Desktop Hydroponic System

The name says it all. This is a very cheap hydroponics system that can be placed on your desk.

The plan is perfect for a small plant, like a herb or lettuce. This ideal for beginners who don't have much space to grow.

The plan involves using a half gallon bucket or even a coffee can as the main container. The plant is housed in a net cup with a growing medium like rock wool.

The most expensive part of this setup is a small bubbler. You can try building this system.

⁇ Mason Jar Kratky Method Hydroponics

This is a low maintenance setup involving no electricity or motors. You have run into the Kratky method from the plan talked above. But this one uses Mason Jar instead of the bucket.

This system requires no special tools or equipment. Most of the components are readily available in homes.

As usual, net cups are used to hold the plants. These are then housed inside the mason jar lids.

The net cups can be homemade using plastic cups that fit into the mouth of the mason jars. The jars are filled with the nutrient solution, and the plant's roots are allowed to grow into it. Perfect for beginners. You can try building this system.

☑ **Dutch Bucket Hydroponics**

Dutch Buckets are also called BATO buckets. These are incredibly versatile containers that can be used in hydroponics systems of varying complexity.

You can easily have a manual watering system where you apply the nutrient solution several times a day to the plants.

Or you can go for a simple recirculating system using tubes, pump, and PVC pipes. To make an automated system, all that is needed is a simple timer.

This grow system can be used for different sized plants. The larger plants can be given a whole bucket, while several smaller herbs can be housed in the same bucket.

Depending on the scale of the system, you can grow a dutch bucket system indoors, or outdoors in a greenhouse/patios. You can try building this system.

☐ Deep Water Culture Hydroponics

If you want to grow stuff like tomatoes and lettuce indoors, this system is ideal. Growers usually use an opaque plastic storage box is perfect as the primary nutrient solution container.

Depending on the size of the box, anywhere from two to eight plants can be grown in this system.

The only other components require are a bubbler and some air hoses to pump in oxygen into the nutrient solution.

The plants can be placed in net pots, underneath LED grow lights. You can try building this system.

⍰ Drip Water Hydroponics

Drip systems can be simple or complex, depending on your requirements and budget.

In a passive system, you can forego the pumps and use gravity to bring the nutrient solution to the plants. This will call for some creative placement of the garden and reservoir.

Or you can just use a submersible pump and a network of thin tubing to deliver the nutrient solution is small amounts to the plants.

A growing medium is usually preferred for drip systems. Popular options include coir and perlite-vermiculite. You can try building this system. This system is on intermediate level.

⚡ Ebb-Flow System

This is another largely inexpensive homemade system that uses a storage tray or tote to house the entire grow operation.

The ebb-flow system involves growing plants in a medium, and flooding the medium with nutrient solution for a few minutes at set intervals. It is also called a flood-drain system. This system is on intermediate level.

This system will need a pump as well as a timer for automated operation. You can try building this system.

16. Stackable Hydroponics

Stackable planters are very popular in smaller gardens to grow a lot of plants in smaller space. But these stacking systems can also be used for hydroponics.

But you will have to factor in the irregular flow into the plants at the lower levels. Stacking is not a very efficient system for hydroponics for this reason.

But it is still worth experimenting, with different plants that have different water and nutrient requirements. You can try building this system.

Conclusion

We have only scratched the surface of diversity in hydroponic systems. Homemade DIY hydroponics is both an art and science.

You can make creative setups that not only produce lush growth but also end up looking aesthetically pleasing as well.

The only limit is your imagination, and of course, the primary concern of getting enough nutrients for your plants.

CHAPTER 4: SUBSTRATES (GROWING SUPPORT MATERIALS)

One of the most obvious decisions hydroponic farmers have to make is which medium they should use. Different media are appropriate for different growing techniques.

Expanded clay aggregate

Expanded clay aggregate

Baked clay pellets are suitable for hydroponic systems in which all nutrients are carefully controlled in water solution. The clay pellets are inert, pH-neutral, and do not contain any nutrient value. The clay is formed into round pellets and fired in rotary kilns at 1,200 °C (2,190 °F). This causes the clay to expand, like popcorn, and become porous. It is light in weight, and does not compact over time.

The shape of an individual pellet can be irregular or uniform depending on brand and manufacturing process. The manufacturers consider expanded clay to be an ecologically sustainable and re-usable growing medium because of its ability to be cleaned and sterilized, typically by washing in solutions of white vinegar, chlorine bleach, or hydrogen peroxide (H_2O_2), and rinsing completely.

Another view is that clay pebbles are best not re-used even when they are cleaned, due to root growth that may enter the medium. Breaking open a clay pebble after a crop has been shown to reveal this growth.

Growstones

Growstones, made from glass waste, have both more air and water retention space than perlite and peat. This aggregate holds more water than parboiled rice hulls. Growstones by volume consist of 0.5 to 5% calcium carbonate – for a standard 5.1 kg bag of Growstones that corresponds to 25.8 to 258 grams of calcium carbonate. The remainder is soda-lime glass.

Coconut coir: Coconut coir Regardless of hydroponic demand, coconut coir is a natural byproduct derived from coconut processes. The outer husk of a coconut consists of fibers which are commonly used to make a myriad of items ranging from floor mats to brushes. After the long fibers are used for those applications, the dust and short fibers are merged to create coir. Coconuts absorb high levels of nutrients throughout their life cycle, so the coir must undergo a maturation process before it becomes a viable growth medium. This process removes salt, tannins and phenolic compounds through substantial water washing. Contaminated water is a byproduct of this process, as three hundred to six hundred liters of water per one cubic meter of coir is needed.[1] Additionally, this maturation can take up to six months and one study concluded the working conditions during the maturation process are dangerous and would be illegal in North America and Europe. Despite requiring attention, posing health risks and environmental impacts, coconut coir has impressive material properties. When exposed to water, the brown, dry, chunky and fibrous material expands nearly three-four times its original size. This characteristic combined with coconut coir's water retention capacity and resistance to pests and diseases make it an effective growth medium. Used as an alternative to rock wool, coconut coir, also known as coir peat, offers optimized growing conditions.

Rice husks

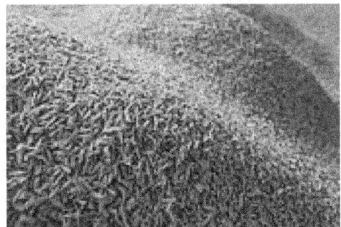

Rice husks

Parboiled rice husks (PBH) are an agricultural byproduct that would otherwise have little use. They decay over time, and allow drainage,and even retain less water than growstones. A study showed that rice husks did not affect the effects of plant growth regulators.

Perlite

Perlite

Perlite is a volcanic rock that has been superheated into very lightweight expanded glass pebbles. It is used loose or in plastic sleeves immersed in the water. It is also used in potting soil mixes to decrease soil density. Perlite has similar properties and uses to vermiculite but, in general, holds more air and less water and is buoyant.

Vermiculite

Vermiculite

Like perlite, vermiculite is a mineral that has been superheated until it has expanded into light pebbles. Vermiculite holds more water than perlite and has a natural "wicking" property that can draw water and nutrients in a passive hydroponic system. If too much water and not enough air surrounds the plants roots, it is possible to gradually lower the medium's water-retention capability by mixing in increasing quantities of perlite.

Pumice

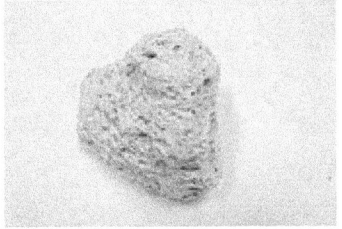

Pumice stone

Like perlite, <u>pumice</u> is a lightweight, mined volcanic rock that finds application in hydroponics.

Sand

Sand is cheap and easily available. However, it is heavy, does not hold water very well, and it must be sterilized between uses. Due to sand being easily available and in high demand sand shortages are on our horizon as we are running out.

Gravel

The same type that is used in aquariums, though any small gravel can be used, provided it is washed first. Indeed, plants growing in a typical traditional gravel filter bed, with water circulated using electric powerhead pumps, are in effect being grown using gravel hydroponics. Gravel is inexpensive, easy to keep clean, drains well and will not become waterlogged. However, it is also heavy, and, if the system does not provide continuous water, the plant roots may dry out.

Wood fibre

Excelsior, or wood wool

Wood fibre, produced from steam friction of wood, is a very efficient organic substrate for hydroponics. It has the advantage that it keeps its structure for a very long time. Wood wool (i.e. wood slivers) have been used since the earliest days of the hydroponics research However, more recent research suggests that wood fibre may have detrimental effects on "plant growth regulators".

Sheep wool

Wool from shearing sheep is a little-used yet promising renewable growing medium. In a study comparing wool with peat slabs, coconut fibre slabs, perlite and rockwool slabs to grow cucumber plants, sheep wool had a greater air capacity of 70%, which decreased with use to a comparable 43%, and water capacity that increased from 23% to 44% with use. Using sheep wool resulted in the greatest yield out of the tested substrates, while application of a biostimulator consisting of humic acid, lactic acid and Bacillus subtilis improved yields in all substrates.

Rock wool

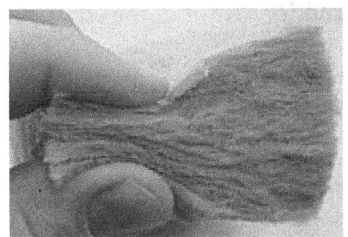

Rock wool

Rock wool (mineral wool) is the most widely used medium in hydroponics. Rock wool is an inert substrate suitable for both run-to-waste and recirculating systems. Rock wool is made from molten rock, basalt or 'slag' that is spun into bundles of single filament fibres, and bonded into a medium capable of capillary action, and is, in effect, protected from most common microbiological degradation. Rock wool is typically used only for the seedling stage, or with newly cut clones, but can remain with the plant base for its lifetime. Rock wool has many advantages and some disadvantages. The latter being the possible skin irritancy (mechanical) whilst handling (1:1000).[Flushing with cold water usually brings relief. Advantages include its proven efficiency and effectiveness as a commercial hydroponic substrate. Most of the rock wool sold to date is a non-hazardous, non-carcinogenic material, falling under Note Q of the European Union Classification Packaging and Labeling Regulation (CLP).]

Mineral wool products can be engineered to hold large quantities of water and air that aid root growth and nutrient uptake in hydroponics; their fibrous nature also provides a good mechanical structure to hold the plant stable. The naturally high pH of mineral wool makes them initially unsuitable to plant growth and requires "conditioning" to produce a wool with an appropriate, stable pH.

Brick shards

Brick shards have similar properties to gravel. They have the added disadvantages of possibly altering the pH and requiring extra cleaning before reuse.

Polystyrene packing peanuts

Polystyrene foam peanuts

Polystyrene packing peanuts are inexpensive, readily available, and have excellent drainage. However, they can be too lightweight for some uses. They are used mainly in closed-tube systems. Note that non-biodegradable polystyrene peanuts must be used; biodegradable packing peanuts will decompose into a sludge. Plants may absorb styrene and pass it to their consumers; this is a possible health risk.

Nutrient solutions

Inorganic hydroponic solutions

The creation of hydroponic solutions simply involves the application of plant nutrition, augmented with deficient nutrient as shown in specific symptoms found in the outmoded soil centered agriculture system. still, the basics of the chemistry relating to hydroponic solutions are distinct from the chemistry of soil in numerous and substantial ways. The key differences are:

- ⬚ In contrast to soil, the nutrients constituting hydroponic solutions have no cation-exchange capacity (CEC) from organic matter. The lack of CEC indicates the Ph level and concentrations of nutrients can be altered considerably more quickly in hydroponic structures than in regular soil.

- ⬚ The Selective absorption of nutrients in most plants is capable of causing differences in the volume of counter ions existing in the solution. As a result, this difference can speedily influence the pH of the solution, including the plant's capacity in the nutrient absorption of related ionic charge. For example, anions of nitrate are usually more consumed by plants in protein formation, with an excess residue of cations in the solution. This disparity in cation likely will cause indication of deficiency in further nutrients centered on cation (e.g. Mg^{2+}), despite a model amount of those nutrients being used in the dissolution of the solution.

? Nutrients, for example, iron can undergo precipitation from the solution, becoming unobtainable to plants based on the Ph or the availability of water contaminants. Therefore, regulation to pH, which includes buffering the solution, or application of chelating agents is sometimes required.

In the outmoded conservative agriculture, nutrients are to be regulated according toLiebig's law to determine the lowest for every plant variety. Regardless, concentrations or absorptions general for nutrient and its solutions do exist, with lowest and highest concentration application for most plants which were comparable. Nutrient solutions are variegated, possessing absorptions in the range 1,000 and 2,500 ppm. Suitable absorptions for the specific nutrient ions that total ppm figure, and are briefed in the table below. The absorptions of necessary nutrients less than these ranges can cause nutrient deficiencies. On the other hand, nutrient toxicity can be caused by exceeding these ranges. Ideal nutrition concentrations or absorptions for plant varieties are recorded basically by practice or by testing the plant tissue before use.

S/N	Element	Role	Ionic FOR	Low range	High range	Common Sources	Comment

			M(s)	(ppm)	(ppm)		
1	Nitrogen	Essential macronutrient	NO_3^- or NH_4^+	100	1000	KNO_3, NH_4NO3, $Ca(NO_3)2$, HNO_3, $(NH_4)2SO4$ and $(NH_4)2HPO$	NH_4^+ interferes with Ca^{2+} uptake and can be toxic to plants if used as a major nitrogen source. A 3:1 ratio of NO_3^- to NH_4^+ is sometimes recommended to balance pH during nitrogen absorption
2	Potassium	Essential macronutrient	K^+	100	400	KNO_3, K_2SO4, KCl, KOH, K_2CO3, K_2HPO4, and K_2SiO3	High concentrations interfere with the function Fe, Mn, and Zn. Zinc deficiencies often are the most apparent.

3	Phosphorus	Essential macronutrient	PO_4^{3-}	30	100	K_2HPO_4, KH_2PO_4, NH_4H2PO4, H_3PO4, and $Ca(H_2PO4)2$	Excess NO_3^- tends to inhibit PO_4^{3-} absorption. The ratio of iron to PO_4^{3-} can affect co-precipitation reactions.
4	Calcium	Essential macronutrient	Ca^2	200	500	$Ca(NO_3)2$, $Ca(H_2PO4)$ $CaSO_4$, $CaCl$	Excess Ca^{2+} inhibits Mg^{2+} uptake.
5	Magnesium	Essential macronutrient	Mg^{2+}	50	100	$MgSO_4$ and $MgCl_2$	Should not exceed Ca^{2+} concentration due to competitive uptake
6	Sulfur	Essential macronutrient	SO_4^{2-}	50	100 0	$MgSO_4$, K_2SO_4, $CaSO_4$, H_2SO4, $(NH_4)_2SO_4$, $ZnSO_4$, $CuSO_4$, $FeSO_4$, and $MnSO_4$	Unlike most nutrients, plants can tolerate a high concentration of the SO_4^{2-}, selectively absorbing the nutrient as needed
7	Iron	Essential macron	Fe^{3+} and Fe^{2+}	2	5	FeDTPA, FeEDTA, iron citrate	Unlike most nutrients, plants can tolerate a high concentration of

#	Element	Type	Ion			Compound	Notes
		utrient				iron tartrate, $FeCl_3$, and $FeSO_4$	the SO_4^{2-}, selectively absorbing the nutrient as needed. [18][61][62] Undesirable counterion effects still apply however.

pH values above 6.5 greatly decreases iron solubility. Chelating agents (e.g. DTPA, citric acid, or EDTA) are often added to increase iron solubility over a greater pH range.[62] |
8	Zinc	Essential macronutrient	Zn^{2+}	0.05	1	$ZnSO_4$	Excess zinc is highly toxic to plants but is essential for plants at low concentrations.
9	Copper	Essential macronutrient	Cu^2	0.01	1	$CuSO_4$	Plant sensitivity to copper is highly variable. 0.1 ppm can be toxic to some plants[62] while a concentration up to 0.5 ppm for many plants is often considered ideal
10	Manganese	Essential	$Mn^2$$_+$	0.5	1	$MnSO_4$ and	Uptake is enhanced by high PO^{3-}

		macron utrient				$MnCl_2$	$_4$ concentrations
11	Boron	Essentia l macron utrient	$B(O H)_4^-$	0.3	10	H_3BO3, and Na_2B4O7	An essential nutrient, however, some plants are highly sensitive to boron (e.g. toxic effects are apparent in citrus trees at 0.5 ppm)
12	Molyb denu m	Essentia l macron utrient	MoO_4^-	0.00 1	0.05	$(NH_4)6$ $Mo7O2$ 4 and Na_2MoO 4	A component of the enzyme nitrate reductase and required by rhizobia for nitrogen fixation.
13	Nickel	Essentia l macron utrient	Ni^{2+}	0.05 7	1.5	$NiSO_4$ and $NiCO_3$	Essential to many plants (e.g. legumes and some grain crops). [62] Also used in the enzyme urease
14	Chlori ne	Essentia l macron utrient	Cl^-	0	High ly vari able	KCl, $CaCl_2$, $MgCl_2$, and NaCl	Can interfere with NO^- $_3$ uptake in some plants but can be beneficial in some plants (e.g. in asparagus at 5 ppm). Absent in conifers, ferns, and most bryophytes
15	Alumi num	Essentia l macron	Al^{3+}	0	10	$Al_2(SO4)$ 3	Essential for some plants (e.g. peas, maize, sunflowers, and

		utrient					cereals). Can be toxic to some plants below 10 ppm.[61] Sometimes used to produce flower pigments (e.g. by Hydrangeas).
16	Silicon	Essential macron utrient	$SiO^2 = _3$	0	140	K_2SiO3, Na_2SiO3, and H_2SiO3	Present in most plants, abundant in cereal crops, grasses, and tree bark. Evidence that SiO^{2-}_3 improves plant disease resistance exists.
17	Titanium	Essential macron utrient	Ti^{3+}	0	5	H_2TiO_4	Might be essential but trace Ti^{3+} is so ubiquitous that its addition is rarely warranted.[62] At 5 ppm favorable growth effects in some crops are notable (e.g. pineapple and peas)
18	Cobalt	Essential macron utrient	Co^{2+}	0	0.1	$CoSO_4$	Required by rhizobia, important for legume root nodulation
19	Sodium	Essential	Na^+	0	Highly	Na_2SiO3,	Na^+ can partially replace K^+ in some

		macron utrient			vari able	Na_2SO4, NaCl, $NaHCO_3$, and NaOH	plant functions but K^+ is still an essential nutrient
20	Vanad ium	Essentia l macron utrient	VO^{2+}	0	Trac e, und eter min ed	$VOSO_4$	Beneficial for rhizobial N_2 fixation.
21	Lithiu m	Essentia l macron utrient	Li^+	0	Und eter min ed	Li_2SO4, LiCl, and LiOH	Li^+ can increase the chlorophyll content of some plants (e.g. potato and pepper plants)

Organic hydroponic solutions

Samples of fertilizers which should be organic are used as enhancements or to completely replace the non-living or inorganic mixtures employed in the conservative hydroponic solutions. Still, the use of these organic fertilizers presents some problems that may be difficult to control. Illustrations include;

⬚ The use of organic fertilizers is very flexible in the

composition of their dietary. Also, there are important differences centered on their sources of related constituents. For example, the animal's diet depends on the value of manure given.

▢ Animal byproducts such as faeces are an important source of organic fertilizers, therefore the spread of diseases from animal to plant have become a major distress to plants supplied for consumption by humans or animal feed.

▢ organic fertilizers or composts usually contain particles that obstruct substrates or various planting gears. So, filtering or refining the organic constituents used to fine powders is usually important.

▢ Many organic constituents, like droppings and offal are decomposed more which produce bad odours.

In conclusion, organic fertilizers are employed effectively in hydroponics if precautions are properly observed.

Organically sourced macronutrients

The following are examples of acceptable constituents for organic fertilizers with their average dietary contents tabulated in relation to percentage of dried mass:

Organic	N	P2O5	K2O	CaO	MgO	SO2	Comment

Constituents							
Bloodmeal	13.0%	2.0%	1.0%	0.5%	-	-	No comment
Bone ashes	-	35.0%	-	46.0%	1.0%	0.5%	No comment
Bone meal	4.0%	22.5%	-	33.0%	0.5%	0.5%	No comment
Hoof / Horn meal	14.0%	1.0%	-	2.5%	-	2.0%	No comment
Fishmeal	9.5%	7.0%	-	0.5%	-	-	No comment
Wool waste	3.5%	0.5%	2.0%	0.5%	-	-	No comment
Wood ashes	-	2.0%	5.0%	33.0%	3.5%	1.0%	No comment
Cottonseed ashes	7.0%	3.0%	2.0%	0.5%	0.5%	-	No comment
Dried locust or grasshopper	Or 10.0%	1.5%	0.5%	0.5%	-	-	No comment
Leather waste	5.5%-22%	-	-	-	-	-	Milled to fine dust
Kelp meal, liquid seaweed	1%	-	12%	-	-	-	Commercial product available
Poultry manure	2%-5%	2.5%-3%	1.3%-3%	4.0%	1.0%	2.0%	A liquid compost which is sieved to remove poison

Sheep manure	2.0%	1.5%	3.0%	4.0%	2.0%	1.5%	Equivalent to poultry manure
Goat manure	1.5%	1.5%	3.0%	2.0%	-	-	Equivalent to poultry manure
Horse manure	3%-6%	1.5%	2%-5%	1.5%	1.0%	0.5%	Equivalent to poultry manure
Cow manure	2.0%	1.5%	2.0%	4.0%	1.1%	0.5%	Equivalent to poultry manure
Bat guano	8.0%	40%	29%	Trace	Trace	Trace	Possesses high amount of micronutrients. Available in commercial quantities.
Bird guano	13%	8%	20%	Trace	Trace	Trace	Possesses high amount of micronutrients. Available in commercial quantities.

Organically sourced micronutrients

Micronutrients are also obtained from organic fertilizers. For instance dung pine bark is rich in manganese and occasionally used in satisfying that particular mineral requisite in most hydroponic solutions. In satisfying requisites for National Organic Programs, crude and rudimentary minerals such as Gypsum and gluconate are supplemented to satisfy the nutritional or dietary essentials of a plant.

Additives/Supplements

Aside chelating means, moist acids can also be supplemented to enhance the taking in of nutrients.

Tools

Common equipment

Towards the success in practicing hydroponic horticulture, achieving ph values and the volume of nutrients must occupy the passable ranges is highly important. The standard tools used in the preparation of hydroponic solutions include:

- ⬚ Electrical conductivity meters: this determines the nutrient ppm by calculating the effective transmission of electric current in the solution.

- ⬚ Litmus paper: this is a disposable paper strip that indicates the concentration of hydrogen ions by color change reaction.

- ⬚ Ph meter: this tool determines the hydrogen ion concentration in solution via electric current.

- ⬚ Graduated cylinders: also known as measuring spoons are

used to ensure accurate measurement during mixing in the making of hydroponic solutions for commercial use.

Equipment

This chemical equipment is used to execute the chemical function of the nutrients of solution accurately. They include:

- Laboratory glassware: pipettes and burettes used for chemical titrations.

- Colorimeters: to determine the color of solution under the Beer-Lambert law

- Balances: used in the correct and precise measurement of materials.

The use of chemical equipment in the practice of hydroponic solutions is helpful to all kind of farmers because nutrients used for the solutions are usually recyclable (i.e they can be reused) and they are almost never totally exhausted. Also, the addition of new nutrients into old solutions saves the money of the farmers and can manage the source of pollution such as eutrophication.

Mixing solutions

Usually, the preparation of hydroponic solutions involving the use of single salts is not practical for small-scale commercial farmers as commercial products are sold at fair prices. Still, when purchasing commercial items, the most popular are the multi-component fertilizers and they are bought in three-part formulation stressing on specific nutritional functions. For instance, solutions needed for enhanced flowering have increased potassium and phosphorus content, solutions needed for vegetative growth have increased nitrogen content and micronutrient solutions containing trace minerals. Another important factor to note is that the application and timing of the multi-part fertilizers is to match the growth stage of the plant.

Before Designing and Building a Hydroponic System

How Hydroponic Gardening Works

Hydroponics are also called hydroculture which involves planting in water constituting a mixture of nutrients. Majority of the foods purchased in markets that we consume are grown with hydroponics, and it is also an excellent method of growing plants in our houses too. These plants are planted and grown in containers made up of water and supplemented with fertilizer in liquid form. Absorption of nutrients by plants occurs after put in water continuously for a period of time from the water. Then, the roots of the plants will naturally adapt and be enhanced to possess a better capacity to store oxygen. After the hydorculture system have been established, all that remains is to observe the water in the reservoir and to determine when there is need for more solution by the plant.

How DOES a Hydroponic System works?

- ? **Reservoir:** this serves as the holding capacity for the water and nutrient solution.

- ? **Air Pump plus Air Stone:** this serves to provide oxygen to the water as it is important in the roots of plants.

- ? **Growing Medium:** this is important as it assists the plants, preferred to garden soil such as small clay stones.

- ? **Nutrient Solution:** this is most important and the micronutrients must complement macronutrients.

Home Hydroponics - a Manual on How to Build Your Own Hydroponics System

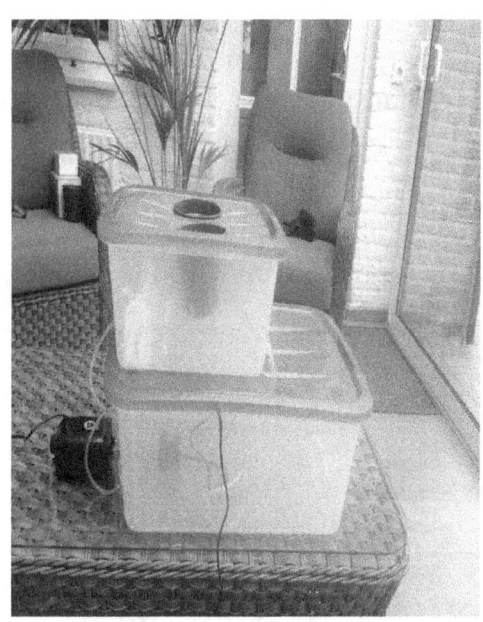

Introduction

Causes and Effects of Overpopulation

The issue of overpopulation should not be handled with levity as it possesses negative effects such as food shortage. It has some terrible effects. The industrial revolution is the major cause of the world's overpopulation about 200 years ago which triggered the global population. This Industrial Revolution increased the growth and transportation of food. During this period, about one billion people were the world's population, but today's current population has increased to over seven billion people.

The population of seven billion people makes it difficult to grow adequate food for everyone, making about 805 million people without having adequate food to sustain a healthy life, and majority of these people live in the continent Asia in mega cities where populations are continually increasing. A mega city is a city having over 10 million people co-existing within its resources, we now have 21 mega cities compared to the 3 mega cities we had about 40 years ago.

How Hydroponics can be a Solution to Food Shortages

In the past few years, the popularity of hydroponics has increased. Defining hydroponics, hydroponics consists of planting without the use of the conventional medium, making use of a water solution rich in nutrients. Hydroponics are small unconventional systems that one plant that can supported with, and even a large quantity of plants, making hydroponics the best way to grow food successfully in our homes. This becomes a major solution in solving the problem of people living in mega cities that find it difficult to get enough food in markets and food stores as they can now grow their own food in the most economical way. As the number of mega cities increase, malnourishment increases as food is a major factor of a good economy. Therefore, they are heavy gains to be reaped from people having good hydroponic systems in their homes. This in turn, will prove most useful in curbing the problem of food shortages in every part of the world.

How to Get Started

Hydroponic systems are sold in many places and on many sites. But, it is better and cost less to go the places to purchase the materials needed to build the systems on your own. Buying the materials needed is more advantageous than buying the kit because one can always make changes to the system at any desired moment and place. One should note that a kit comes with a manual which serves as an advantage. However, below will include instructions and photos to guide one through the setup.

What Method We Will Use

The hydroponics system will take water up from the container which serves as a reservoir through a hose to the area where the roots of the plants are arranged. As water and nutrients are in the container towards the bottom, the roots will carry up the water and nutrients, then the water and nutrients will return to the container or reservoir and the cycle continues. This is known as the NFT method which means Nutrient Film Technique. The NFT is a process of continuous flow of water and nutrients in the roots. The water

and nutrients flow through a pipe but a rectangular container will be used.

What Medium to Use

A number of mediums are suitable to be used in the hydroponic system but in this illustration, clay rocks will be used as the medium because the plant will be supported and there will be enough space between the plants for their roots. Rockwool is an insulator, and it is also a very good medium because it is airy. Airy or light mediums are best for hydroponics system.

How Much Attention is Needed.

If the plants being used have underdeveloped roots, more attention is necessary, especially to assist the roots in the medium and pots in order to get to the water and nutrients. But, with a plant with developed roots, one can pay less attention as one can cautiously pull the roots inside the pots or container until they get to the water and nutrients. The water should be changed time to time to ensure it stays clean. you start out with a plant that doesn't already have developed roots then a lot more attention will be needed because you need to guide the roots though the medium and though the pots to reach the water and nutrients.

Step 1: Materials

Materials

1. Two Containers

One preferably large and deep (this will hold the water and nutrients). Container used was 58 cm x 39 cm x 19.5 cm (length x width x height/depth)

One preferably shallow and the size is related to the number of plants to grow how much plants you want to grow ; 38 cm x 28.5 cm x 17.5 cm (length x width x height/depth)

2. Mesh Pots

The more plants to grow, the more pots will be needed.

3. plants with developed root system should be used rather than seeds or under developed root system.

4. Air Pump

Model: AP-30

Power: 4 Watts

Voltage: 220-240 Volts

Frequency: 50 Hertz

Pressure: >0.015 Mpa

Output: 3.5 liters/minute

5. *Six Meters of Tubing*

6. *Aeration Stones*

7. *A Water Pump*

Model: Aqua-Power 200

Power: 4 Watts

Flow: 200 liters/hour

Maximum Height: 0.60 meters

8. *Medium*

9. *Nutrients*

Step 2: Making Holes for Your Pots

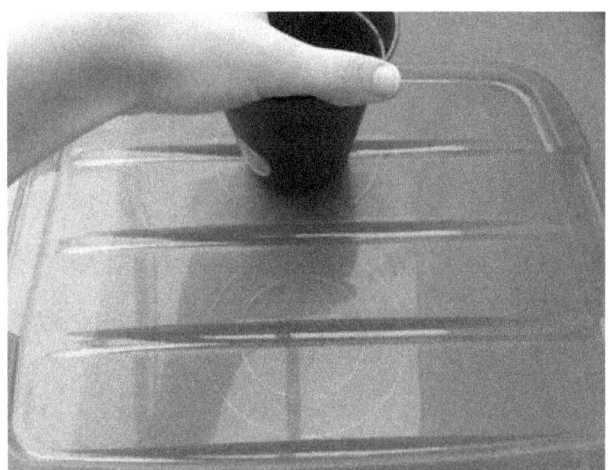

1. Have the lid of the container that you want to put your pots

2. Place the pot upside down on the top of the lid and trace on it to form a circle with a sharp pencil (look at photos for directions).

3. Place the pot right side up on the top of the lid and trace it again with a sharp pencil. This time, make sure this circle is inside the circle of the one you traced while upside down.

4. Repeat this for the number of pots you want to use.

5. At the end, there should be four circles, ending up as two holes. Make use of the images for guidance.

6. Next, drill a hole into the small circle created, use a saw to cut out the smaller circle.

7. After cutting out the smaller circle, start to cut lines that will get to the bigger circle. This will help small attach better to the pots.

8. After that, through the holes, push the pots. If the pots don't fit at first, heat the plastic of the lids, then push the pots into the holes and wait for the heated plastic to cool.

Step 3: Setting Up Your Air Pump

Using some simple tools, one can establish an economical garden that needs little maintenance or management. This garden will be free of dirt and will yield twice more than the conventional garden. This economical garden is based on the hydroponic system and it is very easy and cost-cheap, and it is made easier with these easy instructions.

You can make use of a smaller quantity of water for a test run for the actual container to be used for the hydroponics system, so as not to cause water waste while just testing the air pump.

1. Get a 6 metres length of tubes because tubing will be used along a very long distance. Cut the two pieces of tubes into 80cm each.

2. Before you connect the tubes to the air pump, first plug the air pump into a main socket of electricity and ensure your air pump is actually pumping out air. If it's not pumping, the fan which sucks in the air may be obstructed or the pump may just be faulty. As long as it is not working, don't put water in for safety.

3. Connect the two pieces of tubes to your air pump.

4. Then, you need to drill holes into the container that will contain

the water, after you pass the tubes through the holes.

4. Connect the aeration stones to the same tubes connected to the air pump.

5. Before placing the aeration stones into the water, make sure your air pump is plugged into a main electricity socket.

6. After that, place your aeration stones into the water ensuring they are totally covered by the water.

7. The aeration stones should create bubbles in the water.

Step 4: Setting Up Your Water Pump

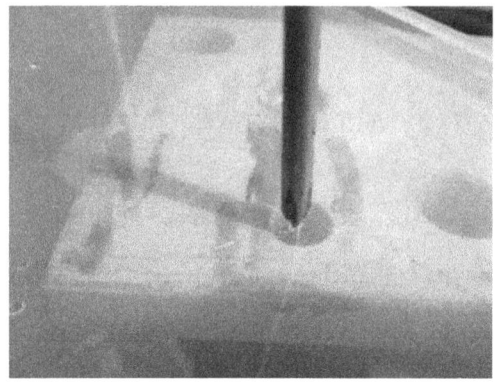

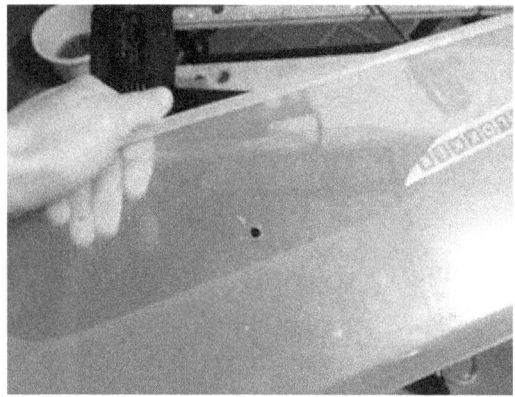

1. First, rinse your water pump with clean water before using it in the hydroponics system.

2. Create a hole into the plastic container to be used for holding water.

3. Then, cut some of the tubes off from the 6 meters and push through the hole created. Connect it with the water pump and container that will hold the pots.

4. If the tubes do not fit in well with the holes, use a very adhesive glue to prevent leakage.

5. Fill the container holding the pots with water and turn the pump on to make sure it is effective by pumping water to the location you want through the tubes.

Step 5: Returning the Water to the Beginning

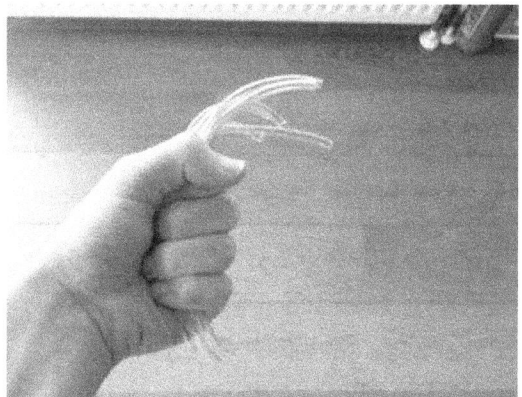

1. Cut the 6 meters tubes into six distinct pieces which should be sufficiently long to reach the water container from the pot container.

2. Create six holes into the pot container and another six holes into the lid of the water container.

3. Place the six tubes into each hole, joining the water container with the pot container.

4. Put water in the pot container, letting it flow via the tubes into the water container to see if it works effectively.

Step 6: A Functioning Hydroponics System

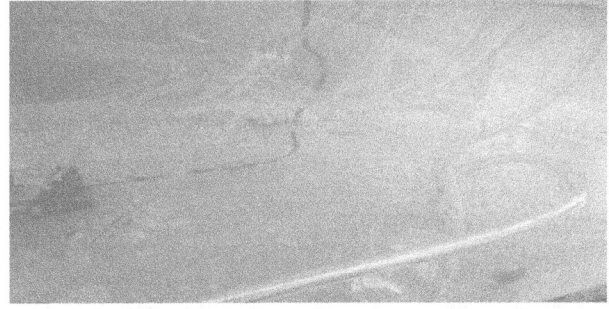

Turn on both pumps after filling water into the water container. At this point, the hydroponics system should be completely functional.

Step 7: Putting Your Plants in Your Pots

1. Start by filling the bottom of the pots with medium spaces left to place the roots in to reach the water.

2. Using lukewarm water, carefully clean all the dirt covering the roots. it is important the water is neither hot nor cold cause this induce shocks to the plants, thereby killing them off.

3. Then, carefully put the plants into the pots, making sure the roots don't come out through the bottom and obstruct the water cycle in the system.

4. Lastly, gently place the rest of the medium needed on top of the plant, and also around it to give the plant base the adequate support needed.

The nutrients added to the hydroponics system strongly depend on the plant being grown. There are general nutrient packs sold that contains the necessary nutrients. Nutrients increase the yield of the plants but there is also a smaller risk for the death of plants using these nutrients.

Step 8: Maintenance

- The water contained in the hydroponic system should be changed once every week as the water could be dirty already. This also should be followed by a replacement of nutrients as they will be lost to the water changed.

- It is advisable to check up on the system a few times daily to ensure the plants are adapting well, and also to observe problems like a leak.

- Lastly, if the plant roots are growing too lengthy and begin to reach the water, they should be planted again so as not to be submerged in the water.

☐ The nutrients shoot out the hole and spray the plant roots. At the same time, the jet of water makes air bubbles so the plants get enough oxygen.

Growing Conditions

Keeping your hydroponics garden inside or outside, it requires a good and controlled environment which is essential to the success of the garden. Three important factors to a successful hydroponics garden include; temperature, humidity and air circulation.

Water and Nutrients Solution

Good water system is vital to a successful hydroponics garden. In conventional soil based gardening, the soil serves as a buffer and filters out impurities capable of causing harm to plants. But, in hydroponics, this filter does not exist as there is no soil, therefore, impurities will have a negative effect on the plants in the hydroponics garden.

Macronutrients

Plants need around 16 mineral nutrients

Propagation

Before beginning the hydroponics garden, the propagation type must be chosen, either seed or seedling and seeds are preferred than the other. You must then choose a method of growing or incubating the seeds or seedlings. You'll have to decide if you're going to start your hydroponic garden using seeds or seedlings.

Medium

Hydroponics do not require soil, therefore, something else must replace the soil to hold the plant system in place. The most preferred mediums are chemically inert to prevent harm to plants, and also inorganic so as to prevent decomposition which could pollute the solution. The medium should be permeable enough to allow adequate water and oxygen get to the plants. Common options used in creating good foundations for plant roots include silica, coco, hydroton.

Ph of water solution

The pH is another key factor in the success of hydroponics gardens. Normal plant Ph is between the range of 5.5-6.5, so the Ph has to be measured accurately. The pH of a solution can be measured with the use of a Ph meter.

Humidity

A regulated humidity is needed as high humidity can kill plants by suffocation and cause the growth of mold around the system. To ensure adequate nutrient intake, promoting good growth and yield, the hydroponics garden's relative humidity should be kept at a range of 40-80%, with best at 50%. Hygrometer is a great tool for measuring the relative humidity of the hydroponics system.

Temperature

Plants need to be away from high hot or cold regions are they are very sensitive to these extreme temperatures. The normal temperature ranges of most plants is between 65-75F. If the hydroponics system consists of a small amount of plants, ample sunlight can be provided via big sunny windows. But for larger gardens, supplement plant lights are necessary to produce enough heat.

Air Circulation

Air circulation is important for hydroponics gardens for a number of reasons. Plants quickly use up the carbon dioxide in air, so there must be a fresh intake of it through fresh air. It also clears away hot or stale air that are capable of suffocating plants. Good air circulation also has an effect on the growth of plants.

Grow Light Systems

Although, plants can do well in hydroponics system with only plenty direct sunlight, additional natural plant lighting is another good way to enhance the system and induce better yield of plants like vegetables and tomatoes. An indoor grow light system consists of four major parts; bulbs, ballasts, lamps and timers. The ballast is the power source and a timer sets the light on for an optimal time of 15-18 hours daily and gives the plant a dark period which in important for their growth and metabolism processes.

A hydroponics gardener could easily purchase a packaged grow light device in the market. These packaged grow light systems or devices are user friendly as they are not difficult to set up to function effectively for the hydroponics garden. Also, a hydroponics gardener can easily purchase the parts separately to make their own custom grow light system. Creating one's own grow light system, it is advised by experts to purchase the individual parts together as each kind of part is made for a particular kind of bulb specifically. For instance, fluorescent bulbs cannot work with an HID part as some HID bulbs cannot work with a fluorescent set up. The following are descriptions of some lights that can be used in creating grow light systems:

Fluorescent Lights

Fluorescent lights are suitable for young plants, young seedlings, especially green vegetables and many herbs. This is because the lights give up a cool intensity with a blue wavelength. For starting hydroponics gardeners, T5's which are mostly made of 12 or 24 inches tubes with 5/8ths inches diameter are the best to be used, they are less costly than others and well known. An advantage of using fluorescent lights is that they don't create too much exothermic heat which makes them very good to use, while a disadvantage is that these lights do not give off enough light power or lumens necessary for a plant's flowering stage.

H.I.D. Lights

High Intensity Discharge (HID) lights are best for growing fresh, round and tasty tomatoes. These lights are very suitable for gardeners with their hydroponics system indoors as they give off the same kind of light that is very alike to natural light (sunlight). A downside to using HID lights is they give off plenty heat and are very costly. The three types of HID bulbs with their advantages are;

⦿ **Metal Halide (MH)**

MH bulbs are capable of creating light that imitates the strength of maximum sunlight and contains plenty of the blue spectrums. This attribute of MH lights makes them very suitable for the growing plants in their vegetative phase, making the plants grow relatively heavy and sturdy.

⦿ **High Pressure Sodium (HPS)**

High Pressure Sodium (HPS) bulbs are better in efficiency to Metal Halide bulbs as they create more light power (lumens), generating a mildly hot yellow or red spectrum of light and this enhances the formation of fruit/flowering, making them the optimal for plants in their flowering phase of growth.

⦿ **Conversion Bulbs and Color Corrected Bulbs**

Conversion bulbs which are also a type of HID bulbs are now the most preferred choice regarding HID lighting. They are also known as color corrected or blue enhanced bulbs. These bulbs are popular because they generate a light which color spectrum contains

appropriate proportions of every color produced. These bulbs are very suitable for the vegetative growth of plants and also promote the flowering phase of plants.

LED Lights

LEDs (light emitting diodes) have been in existence for a long time but started to be used in indoor hydroponics garden only a while ago. Since they have been introduced, they have become well known as they have been proven to highly resourceful, efficient, generating unique color wavelengths necessary to enhance plants vegetative growth and flowering phase, also generating minimal amount of heat. Initial endeavors to use LED lights for indoor hydroponics system were failed as LED lights couldn't generate the necessary light power to enhance vegetative growth of plants. Now, there are new models that have been created that are capable of providing indoor plants with the necessary lumens or light power. If the indoor hydroponics grdener's choice are to use LEDS a try for their system, their selection should have a minimum of 1W per

diode. For instance, a 10 diode bulb must contain a minimum of

10W.

To determine how much light to be used;

For HID light

Formulae= size of garden HID wattage lamp height*cost per 16hours in a day

For T5 fluorescent plant lights

Keep 4-6 inches above the plants always

Make use of 40Watts per square foot of the space of the garden.

Make use of 14 inches' tube per 2 square feet of the garden space.

2' x 2' = 2 4' tubes

2' x 4' = 4 4' tubes

For LED plant lights

The plant light system should have a minimum of 1W/bulb. For example, a 10W bulb with 10W LED lights will have 1W/bulb. you'll want to make sure your plant lights have at least 1W/bulb. If this is not used, the garden will not possess enough light power to sustain the plants.

Growing Tips

Carbon Dioxide

For the photosynthesis process of plants, carbon dioxide, sunlight and water is used to create sugar in the form of carbohydrates which is the source of food for plants. Oxygen is the byproduct of the photosynthesis process and sunlight is a major factor in the process of photosynthesis.

Conductivity

Conductivity of plants refers to the ability of plants to conduct electricity, heat and fluid. To measure the strength of nutrient solution is an easy process and there are electronic devices that have been created to assist in this calculation which used the latest microprocessor technology. But, to use these devices, one must understand that electricity can be conducted by pure water. But when salts are dissolved into pure water, it begins to conduct electricity as the electric current will flow as live electrodes are passed into the solution, pure water becomes the electrolyte of the electrolysis process. The salt solution will get stronger as more salts are dissolved into the solution and more current will flow through to solution. This current flow is to be fixed to a special electronic circuit that will permit the gardener or grower to determine the total strength of the solution of the nutrient.

Electrical Conductivity (EC) or Conductivity Factor (CF) is a scale for measuring the strength of a nutrient in solution and is usually used in hydroponics. It begins from 0 and reaches more than 100 CF units but the length of scale usually used in home or garden hydroponics is in the range of 0-100 CF units, while the scale for large scale hydroponics is between 2-4 CF which could go as high as 35CF estimate for fruits and ornamental trees. However, greater CF scales are made use by highly experienced large scale farmers to achieve unique responses of plants especially for plant hybrids.

Germination

Germination is the process of when a seed breaks out to grow. To germinate means to grow. Seeds are usually germinated within a medium for growing, like perlite. There are many factors involves in this process of germination. Foremost, the seed must be alive and ready to grow and not inactive. Seeds usually have a specific range of temperature that should be established, alongside oxygen and humidity must be available. There must also be a specific level of darkness or light that should be present.

Cotyledons, also called seed leaves are the first two leaves that grow out from a seed. But, these are not true leaves of a plant; they only are sources of food for the developing new plant.

Types of Growing Medium

In hydroponics gardening, soil is never used. Certain growing mediums have the capacity to support nd enhance the growth of plants which permits the roots of plants to have optimal reach to the nutrient solution. Certain media also assist in moisture and nutrient storage while some are best for unique plants and systems. The below are types of Popular growing media:

● Composted bark: this is mostly organic and is suitable for the germination of seeds.

● Expanded clay: these are pellets of clay that are baked in a highly hot oven which produces expansion, making them permeable at the end of the heating process.

● Gravel: gravel add useful minerals to the nutrients and any kind can be employed but, make sure the gravel to be used are clean and free of dirt.

. ● Oasis: these are non-natural and foam based materials.

It is well known for being used in the floriculture as base arrangement.

● Peat moss: this is a medium made up of flattened and carbonated vegetable plant material that have not been completely disintegrated.

● Perlite: perlites are extracted from the lava and are heated in very high temperature in furnaces, making the little quantity of moisture within to enlarge, creating volcanic glass. This process changes the hard glass into little, sponge-like crux.

● Pumice: this is created as a result of volcanic activity, which creates a glassy substance. Pumice is not heavy but light as a result of the release of steam at a very high temperature and heat as the lava rises to the surface.

● Rockwool: this is produced as a result of rock being melted at a high temperature and heat, then turning the melted form of rock into fiber materials.

● Sand: this differs in constitution and is mostly used with a second medium.

● Vermiculite: this is alike to perlites but a difference they possess is the high ability to exchange cation, that is, they can store nutrients for future use.

Hydroponic gardeners are known to be very creative and

experimental persons, so there are plenty other materials that may be used as growing media for the hydroponics system.

CHAPTER 5: MACRONUTRIENTS AND MICRONUTRIENTS

Macronutrients

There are about 16 mineral nutrients important for the ideal growth of plants. But, not all of the 16 nutrients are equally necessary to the plant. There are only three minerals that are majorly needed by plants in high amounts and they include phosphorus (P), nitrogen (N) and potassium (P). They are usually the main constituent of fertilizers made commercially, written in hyphenated valences; "15-30-15", and these valences indicates the relative percentage by weight of the three significant nutrients. These three nutrients; N, P and K are referred to as macronutrient, and they are regularly present in great quantities in plants. Every nutrient is important in yielding healthful plants and produce. Magnesium (Mg), sulfur (S) and calcium (Ca) can also be referred to as macronutrients.

These nutrients play many different roles in plants. Here are some of their dominant functions:

● Nitrogen (N)—helps in the growth of new leaves

● Phosphorus (P)—this is important for the growth of roots

● Potassium (K)—this is necessary for creating plant resistance to diseases and helps in plant growth in excessive temperature

● Sulfur (S)—promotes the dark green color of leaves, making leaves healthy

● Calcium (Ca)—aids the development of shoots and roots of plants.

● Magnesium (Mg)—aids in the promotion of chlorophyll, giving plants the color green due to its pigmentation. Also helps in the assimilation of sunlight in the creation of food.

Micronutrients

Micronutrients exist in scarce amounts in plants and they include; Boron (B), copper (Cu), cobalt (Co), iron (Fe) manganese (Mn), molybdenum (Mo), and zinc. These nutrients are gotten directly from soil, and many of the fertilizers sold commercially do not even contain every of the micronutrients. But, in hydroponics, there is no soil where these nutrients can be gotten for the plants, so, there are specific nutrient solutions that are sold for hydroponics gardeners.

Nutrient Solution

Nutrient solution are most times simply known as nutrients in hydroponics and they are used as plant feed instead of normal water. Unlike hydroponics, conventional plants are grown in soil and get all their nutrients from the soil. Therefore, hydroponics plants need nutrient solutions to survive. In hydroponics, all nutrients needed for the plants growth must be added to the water, thereby forming the solution. The best water for nutrient solution is distilled water. Also, for nutrient solutions, there are different nutrient mixtures for different variety of crops, also depending on their cycles of growth.

In discarding the nutrient solution, one should be cautious of how and where the water is discarded as some can cause displacement in a natural water source such as rivers, lakes or streams if present around the site of disposal. But , if there are no water sources nearby, one can dispose nutrients by pouring in the ground, using them on plants outside or on lawns.

Osmosis

Plant roots and their ends are not as simple as they may look. The extremes of plant roots are not open like hose pipes and do not have the capacity to suck in lots of nutrients. The principle of osmosis hasn't been fully unraveled by science, so describing and explaining the full concept of osmosis is quite impossible. Still, the basic principle of plant osmosis is understandable, regarding plant science.

An illustration; imagine a common piece of blotting paper used for filtration especially in home machines, such as coffee machines. The blotting paper may seem solid but by passing water through one side, water could be seen showing on the other side of the paper, and is as a result of gravity permitting the water to leak to the opposite side of the paper. This illustration is very similar to how a plant root acts.

Through the action of osmosis, plants easily pass through the roots of plants into the plants from the sides, upper and lower regions. Osmosis is the total movement of water molecules from a region with lower concentration to another region of higher concentration due to a natural force, gravity. An easy explanation is simple that greater ion or molecules gets attracted to lesser ions via a semi permeable substance. Therefore, inside cells, there are elements responsible for the attraction of plants roots to water and nutrient solution that is to be passed from the outside region of the plants roots.

To this process of osmosis, nutrients applied to the root of plants do not need to be strong as this could backfire   and cause reverse osmosis. This happens when the nutrients applied to the root of plants is greater than the compounds in the root system. Hydroponics gardeners usually make this error which causes the death of their plants by reverse osmosis. The process of plant osmosis needs to be observed meticulously.

In properly understanding osmosis, the hydroponics gardener can judiciously make use of this learning to induce efficient taking in of water and nutrients without causing adverse effects, like the death of the plants by reverse osmosis, or as a result of too much fertilizing.

Pests and Diseases

Hydroponics gardener also experiences a great number of problems involved in growing plants. Even without the use of soil, pest and diseases still create problems in hydroponics gardens. Pest and diseases are a major problem in farming and plants are the dwelling places to plenty of these plant destroyers. Bacteria like Fusarium, Cladosporium and Verticillium can cause serious damage to plants by stunting its growth process. Also, insects like caterpillars, nematodes, white flies, aphids are also terrible influence to the normal growth of a plant.

These are some ways to protect plants against diseases and infections:

● The growing environment should be kept clean at all times

● Grow plant kinds that is naturally resistant to diseases and infections

● The growing environment should be well ventilated with the right temperature set for plants

● Closely observe the plants and manage problems as fast as they occur

If insects are visibly seen on plants, they should be picked off from the leaves and large ones should be killed. Alternatively, infected plants can be easily cleaned with only water or with a soap that is mild and won't harm the plants.

If the infestation becomes unmanageable by the plants, it may have to come to applying a biological spray to the plants to control the problem. However, pesticides should be used carefully and strictly according to instructions. They are also products that can be purchased in stores that contain botanical compounds that were generated from the material of plants.

On botanical compounds as controlling agents:

Scientific researchers all over the world have been actively researching on compounds in the kingdom of plants that possess the solutions to the problem of infections and diseases in the past few years. These days, almost all pesticide producing companies have started making naturally existing compounds instead of just making artificial pesticides in their laboratories. In doing this, the part of plants like tomato, garlic, lemongrass, neem, derris, have been useful in creating solutions to plant pest and diseases.

pH

The pH of a nutrient and water solution can be described as the concentration of positive hydrogen ions in the solution. Thus, feeding of plants involves an exchange of ions while the negative hydroxyl ions are made by the methods the system filters and air combines with the nutrient solution that plants get their feed. pH increases as ions are expelled from the nutrient solution, which implies that, as plants take in greater ions, the more the plant grows. An equal amount of hydrogen ions and hydroxyl ions exists in the solution with a Ph number of 7. If the solution contains more hydrogen ions than hydroxyl ions, the pH number is less than 7 which makes the solution acidic, while the solution containing more hydroxyl ions than hydrogen ions, the pH number will be greater than 7 which makes the solution alkaline.

To test the pH level of a nutrient, one needs a kit containing testing vials and liquid compounds. These kits can easily be purchased at local market where hydroponics, nursery or gardening items are sold. It is important to test the level of ph of the water before mixing the nutrients to know if the water is acidic or alkaline. If the water is acidic, add alkaline such as sodium hydroxide in bits until equal amounts of acid and alkaline is obtained.

Plant Problems

Constantly, problems arise with the plants and this is very common for any kind of gardening, including hydroponics gardening. Most importantly, the gardener needs to act effectively when these problems arise with good information and resources.

Mineral Deficiency Symptoms

Nitrogen deficiency

Nitrogen deficiency in plants is characterized by the yellowing of leaves from the regular green color, occurring mostly in older leaves. It also causes stunted growth of the shoots and roots and in tomatoes, the stems may even change to a color purple.

A phosphorous deficiency

This deficiency is characterized by leaves turning dark green and stunted growth as in nitrogen deficiency. Also, as in nitrogen deficiency, the stems also change to the color purple. However, the leaves don't take up a yellow color as they do in the lack of nitrogen, the entire plant then changes to a purplish green color.

Iron deficiency

Iron deficiency is characterized by yellow color between the veins of leaves. Comparing it to nitrogen deficiency which the yellowing is dominant in the older leaves, the yellowing starts in the young leaves. If the leaves go on to lack iron for a long period of time, the leaves totally change to the color white.

Wilting

Wilting may be described as a condition which is as a result of disease, usually Fusarium bacteria specie, or environmental agents. Wilt can be counteracted by simply modifying the temperature of the media and nutrient, but the survival rate of the plants becomes low when Fusarium is in control of the plant.

If wilting is due to environmental causes:

Ensure to spray clean and cool water on the plants to rejuvenate the plants. Keep trying if the spraying hasn't changed the plants by the next day.

When changes have been seen in the plants, refill the nutrient solution, then obtain the Ph value.

After applying moisture and there is no noticeable change in the plants, the nutrient tank should be emptied, and top off with a new nutrient solution after changing its location to a more sheltered area.

If wilting is due to a system blockage of nutrient:

Wilting could also be as a result of blockage of nutrients. The plants lacked water and became very dehydrated, so they seemed to have withered away. And when the nutrient was unblocked and it began to flow again, the leaves became hydrated as more fluid passed into it and they returned back to their normal healthy green leaves. Sometimes, the hydroponics gardeners need to understand the true cause of wilt, before taking appropriate actions.

Propagation

Propagation may be defined as the process of multiplying or increasing the amount of plant to be produced. There are a number of ways by which plants are propagated. Hydroponics gardeners can either increase plant produce by planting the seeds, by stem cutting which produces a plant that looks exactly like the parent plant cut from and other methods.

The method of stem cutting isn't effective with all plants but it is still a very effective method. This process involves the cutting off of the top of a major shoot or branch below the growth node. The gardener should ensure that at least two nodes of growth can be seen above the area that was cut. Also, remove leaves that are lower around the bottom of the new plant. After cutting, it should then be rooted by putting it in water or in a moist medium like perlite.

Pruning

Pruning is a process of detaching any plants that is sick, discolored or have been eaten by insects from other plants. This process of removing some of the outer leaves or the top of the plant can help it grow better. Sharp scissors should be used to prune plants and the gardener should prune a lot of the outer leaves so as to enhance growth on the remaining leaves. The act of pruning should be observed with care and caution and roots that are bad, defective or even dying should be pruned regularly.

Soil

Soil should never be used in any part of hydroponics. And, in transferring a plant from the conventional soil based location to a hydroponics system, the gardener should clean all soil and dirt from the plant roots or mixes from the soil because soil contains many microorganisms that could develop and contaminate the hydroponics system. Some of these microorganisms may be parasitic which can inhibit the growth of plants. And this mentioned is another merit of hydroponics as plants in hydroponic systems can grow without being a host to other microorganisms that exist in traditional soil gardening.

Temperature

Temperature differs in different plants as well as different germination. A gardener should ensure the growing prerequisites of each plant are known, particularly the lowest and highest temperature levels. Different varieties of plants possess unique requirements particular to their specie.

Water

Water is an important source of life and nutrients to plants, plants cannot survive without water. The type and quality of water given to plants is very essential and plants depend on their capacity to absorb water easily. Plants absorb water mostly by transpiration in a percentage of 80-90%, compared to animals which absorb by perspiration. Transpiration permits plants to create and also manage its surrounding local climate. It is important that plants have water free from dirt to protect plants against the effects of contaminated water such as diseases, and to create their healthful supply of food.

It is important that water used in hydroponics system be clean and free of pollutants. Therefore, water should be tested before nutrients are introduced, so there won't be addition of an element that already exists in the water. In small scale hydroponics systems, distilled water is the best water to use.

In beginning a large scale hydroponics system, water analysis must be done before use for nutrient solution, and agents such as salt (sodium chloride) and water hardness should be noted. The use of water from the ground, ground water usually possesses elements and ions that are absent in prepared or artificial water. Nevertheless, any water the gardener decides to use must be analyzed and key factors must be understood.

Rooting a Cutting:

- everything needed for cuttings should be available and they should be planted immediately after cutting

- make cuttings early in the morning for optimal results

- make use of healthy plants with soft and green stems as wood stem cutting do not make roots on time

- use a straight and clean cut for soft wood and a slanted cut for brown stem cutting

- cut off branches of leaves that are below the line of soil, cut off leafy stem, remaining ¼ inches stub

- place cutting into root hormone and root the cuttings

- put a some drops of water down to the stem to reach the soil mixture surrounding the stem after planting

To Root in Potting Soil or Soil-less Mixes:

- add potting mix to the containers

- add water of room temperature, also with Nutriboost which is a vitamin mix; seven drops per a litre

- if signs of wilting are noticed, it is advisable to have a "No-Damp" around. make use of the suggested rate of application. Spray No-Damp to 1 litre of water.

- dip your cuttings into root hormones and plant them immediately

To Root in Rockwool Cubes:

- the cubes should be washed in a lukewarm water with a balanced pH level

- nutri-boost solution should be added to the cubes as explained above

- the cutting should be rooted ¾ inches into the rockwool cubes

More Helpful Hints:

- the cuttings should be placed under a normal fluorescent light as 70-75 degree Fahrenheit

- if a clear cover is used, it should be cleaned two times daily against condensation

- the Nutri-boost and water mixture should be used so fresh growth can be seen at the tips of the cutting, then a half strength fertilizer should be applied

Hydroponic Nutrient Manipulation and Modification Techniques

Now, hydroponics gardeners are enhancing the mixes of their fertilizer as mixes without soil, Rockwool and others contain minimal food, unlike dirt in gardens. Therefore, plants respond to any slight change in the power of fertilizers or strength without delay. This creates the major reason why hydroponics gardeners make use of different fertilizers at distinct growth level of plants, ensuring plants have the adequate nutrients and requirements to grow.

Food Strength

Food strength is corresponded to the growing state of plants in the hydroponics garden, also to the condition and activeness of the growing plants.

Weak fertilizer for:

- fresh planted root cuttings

- plants in low light power state

- plants growing in gardens with high temperatures of over 33°C)

- plants affected by diseases, pests, insects etc

- plants in between different phases of growth

- plants in poor growing areas such as poor air ventilation

Regular Strength Fertilizer for:

- plants that are healthy and growing strongly

- optimal temperature, good light and ventilation good

Strong Fertilizers for:

- crop plants with fresh and non-artificial growth spurts

- plants generally in excellent growing state which includes good temperature level, good light supply, good air ventilation, good amount of C02 in the garden's environment, great plant treatment with hormones to enable the plants produce healthy foods.

Note: the food should be increased slowly to prevent shoot tips growing black.

Low Nitrogen Fertilizers:

- aids in preventing "stretching" causing plants to have long and slim stems between phases of growth

- for instance, for a gardener growing chrysanthemum who has reduced the duration of a day to ensure plants begin their flowering phase, the gardener can employ a full power fertilizer containing only nitrogen in order to keep the plants closely packed during up to the formation of the flower or fruit bud.

- the plant's fertilizer should be given at the normal nitrogen rate as soon as the plants enters a new growth phase

Gardeners begin fertilizer application by observing the conditions or states of the garden and their plants, the gardener then have to decide what worth and potency to combine the fertilizers.

So What's the Deal with Pesticides?

Pesticides are quite essential in preserving plants of great worth. These days, pesticides are employed as a last resort to aid plants survival. The aim is to manage the pests and possibly even totally get rid of them.

It is advisable to begin use of pesticides on healthy plants and it has lower risks of developing problems than an infected or diseased plant. Pests usually prey on plants that are not very healthy, sick or diseased. The use of predators is also another way of controlling pests, these predators feed on the pests and when the pest are all gone, they leave or sometimes, even feed on each other. Predators are carnivorous, that is, they feed on meat and not plants, so plants are perfectly safe from them. Predators have been a natural control for pests for ages. Pesticides and rodenticides were employed for the first time during the first world war in France where they were used in their gutters or trenches to manage infestations. Predators are way safer to use cause pesticides in the end create pollutants that pollutes our water, land and even ourselves. Safers and Pokon soaps are great organic methods for pest control, and predators can be easily gotten at the markets. Integrated Pest Management (IPM) refers to the coordinated practices for the economical management of pests with a wide scope of approach.

Avoiding Plant Diseases

When a plant dies as a result of a disease, it is very disheartening to the gardener. Plant diseases are always ready to attack gardens and while some can be easily managed, others are extremely difficult to treat and may requirement repetitive methods of management. For instance, a plant with the mosaic virus will have very slim chances of survival. Plant diseases has effects of plants and production as it greatly reduces crop production despite good recovery rate of plants

Good Growing Conditions and Practices:

The greatest protection against diseases of plants is ensuring the plants are at optimal health and growing at the proper rate, and this is observed by keeping the environment of plants in a great state.

Observation to temperature change, ventilation and changes in air, appropriate spacing of plants, accordant growing environment are all practices essential for attaining healthy plants that will be resistant to pests such as insects, as well as microorganisms causing diseases insects usually attack the least healthy plants ans create more mass people to go on to attack the rest of the plants in gardens.

Sanitization:

Use Healthy Plant Stock

- cutting stock from a diseased plant will only spread the disease to the new plant

- a larger natural resistance to disease is present in a few varieties of plants which is less in their related specie or variety.

Keep Tools, Hands and Clothing Clean

- new host plants can contain diseases, insect eggs and pests which can further spread the pest or disease

- in the process of pruning, transplanting, make sure hands are washed after touched infected or diseased plants before touching the non-infected ones

- make sure tools used are washed or cleaned after each use

- dead leaves should not be kept around the garden

Sterilize Garden or other Grow Media

- this is very essential in the case of using garden refuse or dirt from the yard into the inside containers or employing reused lava rock for new plants

● the potting mixtures without soils and fresh rockwool are seen as clean, so addition treatment is required

Use R/O Water or Distilled

● if there are worries about the availability of diseases or infection in water, there are simple and easy ways of treating water in a way that kills the possible diseases contained. They are:

Chlorine Bleach (1/4 cup for 30 gallons)

○ introduce bleach to water and mix add

○ fertilizer should be introduced to the water after bleach treatment

○ make use of air stone or pump to remove bleach and retain bubbles in water

Beginner Hydrogen Peroxide (35%) (1 tablespoon for 10 gallons)

○ this contains additional oxygen and this oxygen gets rid of diseases present in water

○ introduce to water

○ mix properly, after mixing, fertilizer should be applied

Note: hydrogen peroxide assists plants in absorbing food better and quickly, so this method is of great advantage to plants

Gardeners should closely observe for problems with plants, so diseases and infections can be detected on time and controlled effectively. Diseases are best to be destroyed completely before it takes control and kills off many of the plants in the garden.

Treating Fungus and Bacteria in Your Garden

Seedlings and Newly Rooted Cuttings

- they should be treated with No-Damp and gentle fungicide

- make sure the roots are not dry before roots are drenched

- plants should be treated once a week until they are free of disease

Vigorous Plants - Green Growth (no flowers or crop on plant)

- gentle garden fungicide should be applied on top growth of plants

- all leaves should be made wet as long as the liquid is still on leaves

" Caution " - make sure plants with flowers or yield are not sprayed to prevent burning of yields

● plants should be treated once in a week and the optimal time to spray is in the day so plants can absorb spray in the dark time

Flowering or Crop Plants

● use hand watering benomyl fungicide inside the roots

" Caution " – flowering plants should not be sprayed to prevent loss of crop

● there should be adequate benomyl solution inside the roots to wet the whole system

● the plants should be treated when the roots are soaked from irrigation or feeding and will not be soaked again for a minimum of some hours

● treatment should be applied once in a week

Hints on Treating Plants for Disease

● keep away from high temperature and very strong fertilizers till plants are healthy again

● a plant disease can become resistance of fungicide is used too often, brands should be changed after used for three or four times consecutively.

Light movers

There are plenty advantages to having lights of high intensity within grow rooms and there are many methods to do this. This process of moving the glow of light will eradicate the habit of plants leaning towards the origin of light, and also will produce light to shady places around the light. Given that the light source moves and illuminates, it can reach very near the plants without causing harm to the plant leaves. Light that move is better than static light as they illuminate more space. They also are less costly to use as they do not use a lot of electricity, still promoting maximum growth of plants.

Greater light intensity permits plants to be arranged at a close distance, enhancing more yield and crop excellence. Although, the space in the room, its structure and size will decide the kind of light mover that is best to be used for the requirements of the plants.

Linear movers support the movement of light gradually along the path and they along it again in the same cycle of light. Linear movers are usually six feet in height with only one lamp and should especially be used in growing spaces that are slim and extended.

Circular movers are used especially in spaces of alike length and breadth. They possess a minimum of one lamo and a maximum of three in a circle of 360 degrees. They illuminate a room of ten by ten quarter. This distance can be decreased and hardly ever increased.

The most famous light movers are the two limb and three limb movers; the three limb movers produce more light over the area per square foot. An increase in light concentration indicates that the plants can be arranged at a close distance to each other, therefore enhancing crop production.

Advantages of using light movers:

- an increase in growth over a bigger space

- lamps can be put at a close distance to plants

- there will be a higher plant growth of 40%

- plant stems become more sturdy

- shading of leaves can be cancelled out

- 3 lamps can be attached to circular light movers

- provides products free of pesticides, creating the management of pests

- the nutrient solution can be recycled in a way that it is used in other sites, for example, plants in pots

- media for growing may be used again after first use

- Hydroponics gardening systems require tiny amount of

medium or none at all

- concentrated planting techniques need little space

- arid land can be used for crop production

- induces a total sensitization of the surroundings

- nutrient mixtures best for varieties of plants are different phases

- Plants grown with hydroponics possess high resistance to pests and diseases

- good management of environmental agents produce a greater and highly valued yields

Hydroponics and Economical and Social issues

- hydroponics enhances growth in economy as well as creates a better economy for gardeners, producers, wholesalers and retailers

. - this creates an avenue for job education, opportunities and services

- customer needs are met

Building Your Own Hydroponic System; Hydroponic Pumps.

Basic principals

The leaves of plant need oxygen, carbon dioxide and water while the roots need water, oxygen and nutrients. In the traditional soil system of gardening, plant leeches take up the nutrients from the soil to the roots. The nutrients and water needed are used by the roots to enhance the growth of the plants. The drainage system of soil then permits the water to be restored with air between the spaces in the soil particles and this provides the roots with the oxygen needed. However, in hydroponics system, the nutrients are mixed with water to form the nutrient solution. Instead of soil, a growing medium is employed to provide the roots with the necessary nutrients, oxygen and water. Nutrient solution, also known as hydro juice may be employed to also feed each plant in drops of the solution, and to often totally irrigate the hollow of the roots, then depleted. The two methods need a timer and pump to flow the nutrients inside the roots. hydro juice can also be applied on roots by spraying onto them directly, can also be planted in the nutrient solution. In any of the methods, the rots must be supported at the bottom of the plant stem.

The method of adding drops of nutrient solution will induce the most active increase of growth if every single plant possesses its own drip feed that is constantly dripping. This dripper is situated on roots that is growing out of the bottom of the sprout mass, as the root will become wider, covered with air and solid beneath the dripper. The rate of drip is dependent on pressure but it is usually 4L every 60 minutes' dripper. This rate is a factor to size and length of the tank of drip feed, and the rate will naturally reduce as the solution in tank finishes. A more efficient dripper with a faster rate at the upper end of every side of the root hollows. Plants gardened with this method possess great masses of roots, with only the roots of about three plants taking a quarter of the space in the root spaces. The rate of plant growth will greatly advance by flooding the system at least, every hour of the day.

Starting plants

Some seeds need unique conditions to properly germinate. For instance, seeds of herbs require Many seeds require to be sodden for a period of time. Seeds grown in hydroponic systems germinate superiorly, compared to seeds that are grown in soil.

Planting Seeds

Many seeds are planted just beneath the outside of the growing medium. The advised position is between ½ to 1 inch underneath the soil surface. This position ensures the seeds remain damp and will give it the sensation of the location of light and darkness. The plant root will lean to the dark and the areas with water, also the leaves and stem of the plants.

Seeds such as maize will begin to grow in a period of some days but others, such as bell pepper, herbs and tomatoes will take a longer time to germinate, for a period as long as two weeks. These seeds should be closely monitored by gardeners and irrigated every day, even with no sign of germination. If there is no germination after two weeks, the seeds should be replanted.

Intermittently, if the area of the roots is cold or dried out, germination process will be absent in the leaves.

In growing tiny seeds like herbs, a unique kind of germination can be used. A method is to begin growing the seeds sandwiched between two pieces of article or paper, or a towel saturated with water. The towel is to be moist every day.

Some kinds of seeds and their germination is far more than just dipping them in water. Certain seeds require to be altered in a way to begin the process of germination. Others may just require special levels of light and of temperature. It is important to know the prerequisites of seed before beginning the planting process.

Other Methods of Reproduction

Reproduction with cuttings is suited for some plants. This involves cutting a small portion of the upward top of a plant, removing the leaves under and placing the cut portion to the medium for growth. Examples of plants suited for reproduction by cutting include basil plants are most herbs.

Examples of other methods of reproduction;

Garlic plant is reproduced from single cloves of garlic and not seeds. Therefore, organic garlic are easier to germinate.

In the case of potatoes, they are germinated from the potatoes themselves. The potatoes are grow as a whole or divided into pieces.

CHAPTER 6: HYDROPONICS GREENHOUSES

Definition of a greenhouse

A term that was used earlier recognize a greenhouse was hothouse although the term is not commonly in use as of today. In the Merriam-Webster Dictionary, hothouse is can be defined as "a greenhouse that is maintained at a high temperature especially for culturing tropical plants." A greenhouse is tagged with this identification that is derived due to the fact that it collects beaming energy from the solar that in the interim makes the interior to get heated up. Jensen (2015) defined Greenhouse as '' a structure that is inflated/framed and a translucent/transparent material acts as a covering and allows the transmission of optimal light for production of plants and it also protects against the adversarial conditions of the climate'. Hanan (2014), says that '''Greenhouses assists in the incapacitating the adversity that a change in climate may bring through the use of energy that is free- the SUN''. his identification derives from the fact that a greenhouse will collect solar radiant energy that heats the interior. Jensen and Malter (2015) defined a greenhouse as "a framed or inflated structure, covered by a transparent or translucent material that permits optimum light transmission for plant production and protected against adverse climatic conditions." Hanan (1998) states that "greenhouses are a means of overcoming climatic adversity using a free energy source, the sun." Beytes (2003) defined a greenhouse as "a building having glass walls and roof for the production of plants." That definition would not fit since the glazing (cover) materials in use today include many different types of material other than glass. According to Webster's New World College Dictionary, a greenhouse is "a building made mainly of glass, in which the temperature and humidity can be regulated for the cultivation of delicate or out-of-season plants," a definition that would fit the concept of design and use in this discussion. The term "glasshouse" "is a European term for an artificially heated structure used for growing plants" (Gough, 1993).

A Hydroponic greenhouse has the requisite technology as well as systems that is essential to realise a culture based on the principles of hydroponics and can be defined as an irrigation system in which the plants roots if the crops are balanced in nutrient solutions dissolved in water with all the essential chemicals needed for plant growth, that can be directly grown on the mineral solution, or in a substrate or inert medium(a). Contrasting with traditional greenhouses, most hydroponic systems engage the use of some form of medium to support the plant root. In simple words it means simply growing of your crops in water.

Plants as well as vegetables are positioned in a growing medium such as clay, pellets, rock wool, recycled foam, peat, saw dust, coconut fiber or gravel as well as a fed a feeder or nutrient to aid in their growth.

Plants in a greenhouse can grow all year round. The vegetables, plants/flowers can survive when temperature, nutrients- oxygen, nitrogen, pH as well as carbon dioxide including light are supplied via water.

The supply of the nutrients can be in various forms such as:

Dry, Liquid, Organic blend forms

Water (H_2O) is acquired through reservoirs. Crops can be grown on a salver/tray or in a medium such as gravel/foam blend. There are different farming systems that are in existence in hydroponics:

These hydroponics systems do not have substrates for crop development, and it occurs directly on water-bearing systems by variety of plants such as:

Deep Flow Hydroponics: NGS

Floating systems: Floating Shelves

Systems by water depth: NFT

Aeroponics System

More or less systems keeps the root culture in a container, the whole culture is kept in the dark, where the nutrient enriched solution is applied to the root in form of a mist spray.

Plants are grown in different places such as:

Benches/ grooves crops

Sack growing

Growing in individual containers/channels

Surface crop (sanded)

Furthermore, hydroponic systems can be classified in accordance with the usage of water. They are:

Closed systems

In a closed system, the nutrient solution is recirculated. A disinfection process is required before another set of recirculation is applied. The system of disinfection is the most popular application of chlorine dioxide, ozone, hypochlorous acid or sodium hypochlorite acid as well as ultraviolet radiation.

Open systems or loss solutions

In this system, drains are discarded from the plantation

Benefits of hydroponic greenhouse

- ☐ It maintains optimal conditions for all-out photosynthetic performance.

- ☐ It maximizes the use of energy from photosynthesis which in turn leads to an increase in crop yields

- ☐ It improves the use of water

- ☐ Efficient space usage-The need for a large surface area is not that much unlike when growing plants traditionally.

- ☐ Crop cycles are shortened which leads to accelerated plant growth

- ☐ It brings solutions to issues caused by depletion of the soil while enabling labor use.

Important items necessary for hydroponic greenhouse systems for plants that are suitable

You most likely will have a general idea on the kind of hydroponic greenhouse you would like to have. This would aid in the building of your hydroponic system. For instance, if you would like to grow plants such as kale or argula or even lettuce the fact that they are all leafy greens is what counts. Some plants oulfouor a tray that is deeper for the vegetables roots.

Basic Supplies needed for Hydroponic green houses

There are some supplies that are necessary when building your hydroponic green house. They include:

- A nutrient solution'

- A pump

- A growth medium

- Channels via which water can flow.

- A non-porous growth for instance a vermiculite or a stretched out clay pellets which allows for drainage that is good exceptionally is the base for your plants.

- The growth medium is then positioned into channels or a low-slung pool that comprises the most essential of all the hydroponic supplies- the nutrient solution.

- The nutrient solution: This needs to be a simple food that is needed by the plant that is mixed adequately in a water solution.

Majorly the nutrients preferred for plants are calcium, potassium as well as magnesium but frequently there is addition of other compounds.

This solution shouldn't be submerged fully in the root but flow around them.

There are other necessary hydroponic supplies needed such as a pump as well as ways to regulate the solution pH

Pump: The nutrient solution is continuously kept flowing through the use of the pump which is necessary for the complete process of hydroponics.

A stagnant solution can become stale quickly and end up poisoning the plants

The solution has to be checked constantly to maintain the nutrient levels adequately.

Hydroponic greenhouse space

If you have a greenhouse space already, the space available inside can be assessed. Exact measurements should be taken which includes the height of your greenhouse ceiling.

If you have a sloped roof, the height should be noted at its peak as well as lowest point

There should be adequate space for you to move around

Alternatively, if you don't have a greenhouse, there is an availability of many styles as well as sizes for greenhouses, For instance, indoor as well as mini greenhouses. You should give a consideration to all the ways you can use a greenhouse.

Location Factors

In earlier periods (prior to 1970), greenhouses devoted to vegetable production were located near large population centers, but with the ability to move produce rapidly from one region of the country to another, and even from bordering countries, site selection can be based on factors other than closeness to markets. Jensen (1997) reported on the demise of the greenhouse vegetable industry that once existed around large population centers in the central United

States. He states that "today ... light is considered the most important factor for greenhouse vegetable production, rather than locating close to a population center." Some would dispute this contention, as many single-operator greenhouse vegetable growers are successfully growing and marketing their produce in local markets, which frequently are large population centers. Other than

economic considerations, the location and positioning of the greenhouse can determine how well the enclosed crop performs. Resh (1995) lists the following site requirements:

1. Full east, south, west exposure to sunlight with windbreak on north

 2. Level area or one that can be easily leveled

3. Good internal drainage with minimum percolation rate of 1-in./h

4. Have natural gas, three-phase electricity, telephone, and good-quality water capable of supplying at least one-half gallon of water per plant per day

5. On a good road close to a population center for wholesale market and retail market at greenhouses if you choose to sell retail

6. Close to residence for ease of checking the greenhouse during extremes of weather 7. North-south oriented greenhouses with rows also north-south

8. A region which has a maximum amount of sunlight

9. Not located in an area with excessively strong winds

In addition, the greenhouse should be placed so that features in the immediate area will not shade the greenhouse. Exposure to wind can significantly impact the heating and cooling requirements; therefore, having a windbreak can prove to be highly desirable. In rolling terrain, placement on hill peaks would expose the greenhouse to uncontrollable wind and in the valleys to cool air drainage, fog, and stagnant air. Determining what exists upwind, even several miles away, is important to avoid either dust deposition on the greenhouse or the possible intake of substances that would cause damage to the enclosed crop. If the greenhouse is to be placed in an actively cropped area, what crops are being grown and what chemicals are being applied to these crops must be known. Some crops, such as soybeans for example, are excellent insect hosts; insects can be brought into the greenhouse through the ventilation system, thereby adding to pest control requirements. Herbicides and other pesticides applied aerially to nearby field and fruit crops can be carried by drift into the greenhouse through the ventilation system. Having a windbreak can minimize the deposition of suspended material that might accumulate on the greenhouse surface or the immediate surrounding area. The author visited a large greenhouse complex that was located in an isolated area where there was little human activity within miles. Selecting such an isolated location would minimize what might be brought into the structures from surrounding human activity. In addition, the immediate area around a greenhouse must be kept as inert as possible, with the minimum of activity from operations that might stir up aerial particles, such as having nearby service buildings bringing vehicular traffic close to greenhouse entrances. At one time, the author was responsible for a series of research field plots at various locations. At one location, a site east of a heavily traveled highway, the yield results were consistently different from those obtained at the other locations. It was not until I measured the amount of ammonia (NH_3) in the atmosphere above the plots that I understood why the yield results at this site were always higher. The NH_3 that was coming from truck and automobile exhaust was being deposited on this field plot as ammonium-nitrogen (NH_4N), which contributed sufficient N to the crops being grown on these plots to significantly influence yield.

The author was curious why a large greenhouse operator selected a certain area in the southeast for the production of foliage plants. Besides the availability of an educated work force and a desirable living area, the specific location was determined based on long-term weather records that showed the number of cloudless days during the year for that area was high. A similar greenhouse location in upstate New York was selected since the daily light conditions based on long-term sunshine data records were higher for that particular site than that for the surrounding area. Based on solar photosynthetically active radiation (PAR), Table 12.1 being the "most important factor for greenhouse vegetable production," Jensen (1997) suggests that the southwestern desert regions of the United States would be an ideal location, and indeed such placement and growth in acreage has occurred in that area.

Basic Structural Design

The structural design of a greenhouse is critical as the size and spacing of framing material can affect the extent of light shadowing, while some types of structural materials can act as thermal accumulators, adding either desired or undesired heat to the greenhouse atmosphere. The ability to withstand wind and snow loads will determine the strength required for the structure, an important consideration in some areas. A common error made in greenhouse design is to underestimate the impact of extreme climatic events (wind, hail, and snow) on the structural integrity and maintenance of the interior environment. Commonly used structural materials are treated wood, galvanized steel, aluminum tubing, and PVC tubing. Greenhouse structures vary from just a loose covering over the top of the crop (Wells, 1996), with or without moveable side curtains designed to protect plants from rain or from the extremes of outside temperatures, to a relatively airtight structure so that the interior environment can be precisely controlled. Polyethylene film-covered greenhouses normally have rigid clean plastic (polycarbonate) end walls. Quonset (trademark for prefabricated shelter set on a foundation of bolted steel trusses and semicircular arching roof) is the common design for polyethylene film-covered structures. A single-bay commercial greenhouse structure can vary considerably as to physical size: length 90 to 130 ft (27.4 to 39.6 m), width 24 to 40 ft (7.3 to 12 m), and height 8 to over 12 ft (2.4 to 1.6 m) to the gutter. The height of the greenhouse can have a significant effect on the ability of the heating and cooling systems to maintain a uniform air temperature within the structure. The larger the volume of air to be conditioned tends to minimize significant shifts in the interior air temperature, humidity, and CO_2 concentration. Gutter-connected greenhouses offer economy in construction and space utilization but add additional requirements to control the interior environment. Large open areas pose challenges for disease and insect control as well as special equipment to maintain uniform atmospheric conditions throughout the structure. The design of entrances and the placement of screen coverings over air vents and other openings will determine how well insect and disease organisms can be kept from entering the greenhouse (Jacobsen, 2003). The main door entrance into the greenhouse should be housed in a doored attachment, similar to entrances into most business buildings. Entering the attachment, workers can change clothes, walk into a disinfectant bath, etc., and then enter the greenhouse without a blast of air being injected into the greenhouse if the ventilation fans are operating. How well the various sections of the greenhouse fit together will determine how "tight" the structure will be, a desirable feature to keep unwanted air and insects out, but if it is too "tight," uneven air pressure from inside or out may result in cracks and breakage of joined sections. For glass- or rigid plastic-covered greenhouses, such structures frequently have moveable vent panels at the rigid line, or large moveable vents that can open the entire top of the greenhouse. For most plastic film-covered greenhouses, the common design is to place an exhaust fan(s) at one end of the greenhouse (Figure 12.6) and an adjustable opening, with or without a cooling pad (Figure 12.7), at the other end so that air can be pulled through the length of the greenhouse. Air baffles may be placed at various positions in the gable so that air being pulled through the greenhouse by an exhaust fan(s) will be periodically directed downward, ensuring air mixing throughout the entire depth and length of the greenhouse. A very effective way of ventilating a greenhouse is to place the ventilation fans and cooling pads on opposite sides along the length of the greenhouse so that air is pulled across the shortest distance. Unfortunately, few greenhouses are so designed.

Flooring

A range of materials can be used as flooring in the greenhouse; the best choice is concrete, and the least desirable choice is compacted soil or sand. For initial cost considerations, the walkways may be concrete, while the crop rows consist of sand or gravel or other similar materials. The crop rows and, if the entire floor consists of these materials, other than concrete, plastic ground cover should be placed over the crop rows or the entire floor to serve as a barrier. Crop trash, a source of disease and other problems, that falls on an open floor cannot be taken up if the floor is not firm. The lack of firmness of the flooring can cause problems with use, affecting foot traffic movement in the greenhouse as well as interfering with the floor drainage system. With a smooth and firm flooring material in place, keeping the floor clean and free of trash is greatly enhanced.

Glazing Materials

Glazing simply refers to the type of material covering or attached to the greenhouse frame. Another term that is found in the literature for glazing is cladding (something that covers or overlays, according to the Merriam-Webster dictionary). The commonly used glazing materials are glass, polyethylene film (high or low density, linear low density), ethylene vinyl acetate, and coextruded films. At one time, fiberglass was frequently used, but its flammability has almost totally eliminated its use today. Coene (1995) lists five important considerations when selecting the greenhouse covering:

1. Material integrity in direct sun without losing clarity

2. Guaranteed lifespan

3. Fire resistance

4. Transmission of photosynthetic radiation (PAR)

5. Energy efficiency properties

Another characteristic is the diffusion of light passing through the covering. Light diffusion will distribute light more evenly in the greenhouse, resulting "in more even light distribution without defined shadows" (Coene, 1995). Fiberglass has a high diffusion property as well as structural strength; for these reasons it was, at one time, in wide use as a glazing material. Some types of coverings will not transmit equally all the wavelengths of light striking their surface, thereby filtering the light and changing its spectral characteristics (Morgan 2003a). The characteristics of various types of glazing materials including glass, polyethylene film, polycarbonate, fiberglass, and acrylic are discussed in the book edited by Beytes (2003a). All these materials have varying transmission characteristics that will significantly affect radiation input and output from the greenhouse. The selection of which glazing material is best will be determined by cost, durability, and external environmental factors (i.e., wind, snow load, hail resistance, etc.). The so-called "greenhouse effect" is a phenomenon due to a shift in wavelength. Radiation entering the greenhouse adds heat to the interior environment due to a wavelength shift, as radiation reflected back from the interior surfaces is of a longer wavelength than that entering and is therefore trapped within the greenhouse as heat. The effect of light filtering and diffusion on plant color and architecture was illustrated to the author in a greenhouse tomato experiment conducted in two greenhouses that were located just a few miles apart. One greenhouse was covered with fiberglass, the other glass. Those plants in the glass-covered house were dull green in color and had long internodes, while those in the fiberglass-covered house were dark green in color with short internodes. Interestingly, only small differences in fruit yield occurred, but the tomato plants in the glass-covered greenhouse required more frequent adjustment due to their longer internodes.

Heating and Cooling Heating and cooling requirements will vary depending on the location, type of structure, and crop to be grown (Anon, 2019). In general, it is better to oversize these systems in order to ensure that the environment inside can be easily maintained. The positioning of ventilation fans, cooling pads, and heating devices will determine how well the inside air temperature and humidity can be controlled. For some crops, such as tomato and cucumber, air movement up through the plant canopy is preferred. Floor heating, particularly in cooler climatic areas, can be beneficial to a crop, keeping the rooting medium at or near the ambient air temperature in the greenhouse. The warming of the nutrient solution/water to that of the current air temperature in the greenhouse, or even 4 to 5 degrees F above the ambient air temperature (Smith, 2002b), will minimize possible plant wilting due to reduced water uptake. The rate of water uptake by plant roots is correlated to temperature, decreasing with decreasing temperature (Nielson, 1974; Harssema, 1977).

Heating

There are primarily two systems for heating the greenhouse atmosphere, forced hot air or radiant heat. The most commonly used is either a natural gas- or propane-fired jet fan heater placed in the gable of the greenhouse on the ventilation fan end. Heated air is pushed through a gable-placed large plastic-holed tube running the entire length of the greenhouse The heated air is distributed through the holes in the tube, the force of the discharge being sufficient to push heated air into the greenhouse cavity. The burning of fuel in the greenhouse adds humidity to the atmosphere. When the outside temperature cools the supporting greenhouse structure, the moisture will condense, making the walls and interior structures wet, including the plants, which is highly undesirable. The other heating method is by the passage of either boiler-generated hot water or steam in pipes that are placed down the sides of the greenhouse at floor level, and in some instances, pipes are placed between crop rows. This type of heating system is referred to as "hydronic heating"; it provides even heating of the greenhouse atmosphere by radiation from the heated pipes. With hydronic heating, the greenhouse and canopy atmospheres are kept dry as heated air moves from floor-level pipes through the plant canopy into the gable. Using a small gable-placed fan, this moisture-laden air can then be exhausted out of the greenhouse.

Heat loss from the greenhouse occurs by three processes: conduction (heat loss conducted through solid materials), convection (removal of heat by air currents), and radiation (heat loss by short or long wavelength radiation through the glazing material). In addition, heat loss can occur through infiltration of cool air and loss of heated air through cracks and openings in the greenhouse.

Air Movement

Air movement throughout the greenhouse, and particularly within the plant canopy, can have a significant effect on plant performance. In an enclosed greenhouse, air movement created by the operation of heating and/or cooling equipment may not be sufficient to thoroughly mix the air in the entire greenhouse (Short, 2003). Even the placement of fans in the greenhouse gable directing air into the plant canopy can be ineffective. With a dense plant canopy created by tomato and cucumber plants, for example, it is very difficult to push air into the canopy, as the canopy acts like a "box," and air movement directed at the canopy either passes over the top or glances off of it. Therefore, the air within the canopy has characteristics (temperature, humidity, CO_2 content) of its own which can be quite different than those of the air surrounding the canopy. The only way that sufficient air movement can be obtained is by the introduction of moving air from the base of the canopy so that air is constantly moving up through the canopy. This air may be conditioned, that is, either heated or cooled. If no air is being brought into the greenhouse from outside, it is very important that the entire mass of air within the structure be constantly mixed as plant growth and function can be impaired by standing in still air.

Plant Support System

For tomato, cucumber, and pepper greenhouse production, a plant support system must be installed. The system usually consists of a strand of strong wire stretched over the plant row with hanging string attached to the wire at each plant location. The plant is tied to the string. Various systems have been devised to ensure that sufficient string is present at each plant location to provide for lowering and tying over a full season of plant growth. The attachment of the support wire to a structural greenhouse member is not recommended since the plant weight on a support wire can be several tons. Most greenhouse structural members are not able to hold such weight. The support wire should be attached to sturdy-set stanchions placed about every 30 ft (9 m) down the plant row, or the stanchion can be placed in the middle of a double row with a cross piece at the top to hold each support wire in place.

Supplemental Lighting

There are two primary reasons for supplying supplemental light: photosynthetic, utilizing light sources to provide part or all that necessary for normal plant growth, and photoperiodic, that required for controlling flowering and plant shape (Sherrard, 2018). For many plants, the quantity of light for photosynthesis ranges from 100 to 1000 times that needed for photoperiodic lighting. If used for either application, the cost for supplemental lighting should either be equal to or less than the financial return gained by its use. For photosynthetic effect, supplemental lighting to extend the hours of daylight may be its only legitimate use for most crops. Supplemental lighting to increase light intensity during daylight hours is highly questionable in terms of significant benefit measured by increased yield and quality of produced product. The light level in the greenhouse to sustain growth for tomato and lettuce, for example, ranges between 800 and 1200 foot candles. The light requirement of plants varies considerably and those plants that are highly light responsive can benefit from supplemental lighting.

Controlled Environment Agriculture Systems

Commercial Structures

Today's commercial greenhouses are constructed of galvanized steel, extruded aluminum, fibreglass, polycarbonate, acrylic, polyethylene and glass. The percentage of each, comprising a typical structure, varies by type of design.

Loosely categorized, the following basic shapes and styles are prevalent:

● freestanding grade to grade hoop houses (quonset) clad in polyethylene, double polyethylene, corrugated fibreglass sheet, or plastic composite structured panels

● linked or gutter-connected straight-wall hoop houses clad in polyethylene, double polyethylene and so on as above

● linked or gutter-connected straight-wall hoop houses clad in curved automotive glass

● linked or gutter-connected straight-wall peaked houses clad in flat tempered glass. This style of range breaks down into three further subcategories: - single peak gutter-to-gutter - double peak with floating gutter - triple peak with two floating gutters

All of the above styles or designs of greenhouses are popular, the grower selecting which he will build based on crop to be grown, usage pattern, seasonal pattern, as well as economic considerations.

● Nutrient control insures that the plants get the minerals they need at the right pH and temperature.

● Faster growth then soil grown plants.

● No weeds. The medium is mostly inert and unless it is out doors, there is no way for weed seeds to get into the growing medium.

Controlled Environment Agriculture (CEA) Controlled environment agriculture (CEA) is a science that describes systems of protected agriculture for the ultimate in environmental control at both the aerial and root levels. Such systems are found in many greenhouses and for all totally enclosed structures. The range of control includes air and root temperature; atmospheric humidity; atmospheric gas composition; light intensity, wavelength composition and duration; water supply and quality; growing medium; and plant nutrition.

The Hobby Greenhouse

For the hobby grower, having a greenhouse structure for use in the cool or cold seasons of the year provides enjoyment as well as the ability to grow plants either for beauty or to provide a supply of off-season vegetables. For some, the greenhouse may only be used to start plants for summer growing or to extend the growing season for potted plants. The author knew an Ohio resident who wanted a fresh rose on her breakfast table every morning, a feat that required considerable skill and the requirement of a greenhouse for flower production during the winter months. Beginning with a small greenhouse, hobbyists can determine whether they have the desire and skill to enter into the commercial production of plants at some future time. There are many structural choices in the design, size, glazing, and control features available for hobby greenhouses (Knutson, 1997). The greenhouse may be attached to another building (home, garage, or outbuilding) (Johnson 2002a) or be a window greenhouse or a stand-alone structure. Depending on the size and type, the greenhouse may be a solar house (Kubiac, 1999b; Johnson, 2000b; Garzoli, 2001), or one with heating and cooling capabilities in order to precisely control the interior environment. Bartok (2000) has written an excellent manual to guide users in determining what type of structure will best meet their need and then provides instructions on how to successfully manage a greenhouse. Bartok (2000) describes six greenhouse styles:

Gable (sloping, flat roof panels and vertical sides) Slant-leg (flat, sloped roof panels attached to a sloping side wall) A-frame (easy-to-build style) Hoop (formed by covering bent pipe or tubing with a flexible plastic cover) Gothic (roof and walls form a continuous shape).

Solar Greenhouse

A greenhouse is an excellent solar collector as entering radiation energy will warm the interior, giving rise to the term "hothouse" as a definition. Therefore, any greenhouse structure could be termed as being "solar." However, the term "solar greenhouse" normally refers to a structure that is entirely heated by solar means. For the solar greenhouse, its climatic location (solar energy input) and placement, glazing, and sun angle and the use of heat-storage devices can determine how efficiently the house will perform (Bartok, 2000). The books by Yanda and Fisher (1980) and Fuller (1999) describe the design, construction, and operation of a solar greenhouse. Johnson (2002a) describes the requirements for building a passive solar greenhouse with "glazing oriented toward the southern exposure of the sun in the winter when the sun is low in the sky." The glazed wall should be oriented directly at the sun at noon on December 21. In a Virginia Gardener Newsletter, it was stated, "the area of glazing should collect enough heat during a clear winter day to keep both the greenhouse and adjoining space at an average temperature of 60 to 70°F (15 to 21°C) during the day." In colder climates, double glazing of the solar greenhouse is recommended, plus the use of thermal blankets. Yanda and Fisher (1980) advise that "a side view of the greenhouse cut out of paper is helpful in determining light patterns through clear roof areas and sides" (Figure 12.21). "By repositioning the solid/clear areas in the model, one should be able to get maximum winter sunlight for your location and also obtain some summer shading." Garzoli (2001) describes various solar means of heating a greenhouse with the use of solar collectors to heat air or water, and then storing the heat generated for later use. Various passive systems are also described for collecting, storing, and using heat.

An efficient solar greenhouse has sufficient thermal mass (water and rocks are the most commonly used primary collectors) to collect, store, and then release the collected passive solar heat at night. The darker the color of the thermal collector, the more efficient it becomes. In cool and cold climates, the nighttime temperature can drop to between 40 and 45°F (4.4 and 7.2°C); therefore, additional heat may be necessary to keep certain plants healthy and productive. Since passive solar greenhouses will be warmer in the summer and cooler in winter than conventionally heated or cooled greenhouses are, crop selection must be confined to those crop species with wide temperature tolerance. During the day on bright sunny days, the air temperature may reach 85 to 90°F (29 to 32°C), while the nighttime temperatures may drop to 40 to 45°F (4.4 to 7.2°C). Johnson (2000b) lists from excellent to poor the suitability of crops for a solar greenhouse:

If air temperatures can be maintained away from the extremes given above, crops such as cherry and large fruit tomato, European cucumber, and pepper can be successfully grown in a passive solar greenhouse or if some degree of temperature control is used.

Common Errors Made in the Design and Operation of a Greenhouse

1. Failure to take into consideration extremes in weather events (i.e., wind, snow, and hail) in the design and strength of the physical structure

2. Site selection that fails to take into consideration the surrounding environment

3. Failure to keep the area around the greenhouse free from substances that might enter the greenhouse and damage the

enclosed crop

4. Undersizing heating and cooling systems

5. Failure to keep the greenhouse structure in a high state of repair

6. Inadequate control of the entrances, thereby allowing pests access to the greenhouse

7. Failure to adequately sanitize the greenhouse between crops

8. Inadequate control devices that do not respond quickly to changing conditions inside and outside the greenhouse

9. Lack of fail-safe or backup devices to maintain the greenhouse operation during periods of extreme weather conditions, power failures, mechanical failures, etc.

10. Lack of alarm systems to alert the greenhouse manager of a problem when off site

11. Not being proactive in the control of insect and disease infestations

12. Failure to utilize professional resources particularly for identifying and applying control measures for disease and insect infestations and nutritional problems

13. Failure to use strict criteria in the selection of greenhouse managers and workers

14. Lack of a continuous training and supervision program for greenhouse workers in the techniques of greenhouse operations and proper crop management procedures

15. Failure to adopt new technology promptly

GROWING

MARIJUANA

FOR BEGINNERS

BIBLE

Growing marijuana the beginner's Bible: A step by step guide that teaches you what the new techniques of indoor and outdoor cannabis farming are, both for personal use and medicinal, and what the secrets are for fast and pure cultivation.

JHONNY GREEN

CHAPTER 1: MARIJUANA HORTICULTURE

Marijuana (Cannabis) belongs to the genus in the plant family Cannabacea which includes three other species *C. sativa, C. indica* and *C. ruderalis.* The plant is usually a fast-growing, annual and dioecious (a plant group that usually includes distinct male and female group) unless it is epigenetically hermaphroditic. Such hermaphroditic varieties are most common among some varieties native to south Asia but can also result from environmental stress such as inadequate light or nutrition. Cannabis is wind-pollinated and produces "seeds" that are technically called achenes. Most strains of Cannabis are short day plants, with the possible exception of *C. ruderalis* and some equatorial *C. sativa* varieties that are commonly described as "auto-flowering" and may be day-neutral. Cannabis plants produce a group of chemicals called cannabinoids which are secreted by glandular trichomes that occur most abundantly on the floral calyxes and bracts of female plants.

Cannabis plants evolved from and are indigenous to Central Asia, Himalayan foothills and the Indian subcontinent. However, the use of cannabis and its products spread quickly throughout the world and is now cultivated in climatic zones from the Arctic to the equator. Varieties of marijuana strains are developed by breeders to strengthen certain characteristics of the plants. *C. sativa* is reasonably tall (could reach as high as 4.5 metres). It possesses long internodes and branches with large narrow-bladed leaves which bloom later than *indicas*. On the other hand, *C. indica* varieties are shorter, wilder and have broader leaflets; they also often mature a month or two faster than *sativas*. *C. ruderalis* is a very short variety due to its auto- flowering traits.

Sativa Variety

Indica Variety

Also, apart from height, width and branching traits, marijuana varieties differ in many ways especially regarding growth characteristics such as: leaf size and shape, flowering time to yield, potency, taste and aroma.

MARIJUANA GERMINATION

Germination is the process in which a new plant begins to develop from a seed. Marijuana germination is the process of seed sprouting. Also referred to as popping, this is the first stage in marijuana gardening. In this stage of cannabis horticulture, after about 3-7 days, the seedlings sprout little white-coloured tendrils and begin to establish their root system. These white-coloured tendrils that sprout during germination are the plants' very first roots, also known as a taproot. All other roots yielded by the plant during its lifespan will sprout from the taproot. In other words, a sole taproot is produced from the seed germination as it grows into the soil or growing medium and then the root systems begin to branch out. While the rootlets grow below the surface, the stem branches upwards in its search for light. These tiny rootlets extract water and nutrients needed for the plant's survival. Hereby, conveying the water and nutrient solution to the leaves which the leaves in turn convert to sugar to ship to the roots. Roots also serve as an anchor to the plant in its growing medium.

During germination, moisture, heat and air activate hormones (cytokinins, gibberelins and auxins) within the durable outer coating of the seed. Cytokinins promote lateral growth and allow more cells to form (cell division) while gibberellins increase cell size and directs stem and leaf growth. The primary function of the central stem is to transmission of water from its delicate root hairs up and throughout the entire marijuana plant. Lateral and side branches begin to branch out to develop buds and leaves to enable photosynthesis. Auxin is found in the growing tips of both the roots and the stem.

It directs orderly new growth and develops the shape of the plant by inhibiting growth of the lower branches. Together, these plant hormones induce germination. After the activation of hormones, the plant's embryo expands, nourished by a supply of stored food within the seed. Seedlings should receive 16 – 18 hours of light to maintain strong healthy growth. As soon as plants germinate, they require light. If the light is not intense enough, the stem stretches, reaching for it. Cannabis seeds need only water, heat and air to germinate. Seeds sprout without light in a diverse range of temperatures; from 70-90F (21-32C). However, when germinated seedlings lack moisture, their growth is stunted.

Seedling with the cotyledons (embryonic leaves) and first set of true leaves

Seedlings transplanted to 3-gallon containers.

As mentioned, the marijuana plant needs some vital elements to get the best germination returns. The basic necessities of marijuana are:

☐ Light

☐ Air

☐ Water

☐ Nutrients

☐ Warmth

Light

Marijuana plants utilize light for several purposes during germination including the regulation of life processes such as the initiation of flowering. Light can be natural (outdoor growing) or artificial (indoor growing). Light and water are vital to enable the plant to convert carbon dioxide into oxygen necessary for plant growth; this is called photosynthesis. Although marijuana seeds do not require much lighting during the initial germination process, it becomes a necessity the moment the cotyledon appears. In addition to using light for energy, marijuana plants use it to regulate growth.

When marijuana plants lack adequate lighting, they form fewer side branches and elongate abnormally. This abnormal elongation causes marijuana plants to grow tall so as to grab enough light in nature. Plants that receive enough light grow wider (not taller) and produce a flurry of lateral branches with a mass of buds. Hence, whether stems are elongated or stout is determined by light. Under artificial light, the marijuana plant typically need about 16 – 24 hours of light and 0-8 hours of darkness from germination to flowering. Longer light periods are more conducive to vegetative growth while longer darker periods are conducive to flowering.

Marijuana plants growing in unobstructed sunlight

Marijuana plant growing indoors under amber coloured lamps'

However, the best source of light is the sun and marijuana is a sun-loving plant. It grows fastest and is most potent when it gets unobstructed light all day.

Air

Good air flow within the growing space is important to the plants' health. Plants depend on the air movement to grow strong and vigorously. Marijuana seeds need air to germinate because without air currents, the leaves' rough surface and tiny hairs trap the air in a micro-environment that differs significantly from the surrounding atmosphere.

Marijuana depends on air currents to move air and renew the micro-environment. When it is not moved vigorously, the growth rate slows and the micro-environment remains CO_2 depleted. As plants sway with the wind in an outdoor environment, they develop tiny breaks in the stem. The plants repair the damage quickly by reinforcing the breaks and tears, leaving them stronger and stouter than they were originally.

Water

First, hard marijuana seeds are soaked for up to $24 - 32$ hours so moisture can penetrate the protective seed shell. Once a seed receives moisture, it needs a constant stream of moisture (water) that will transport nutrients and hormones to carry on plants development.

However, watering frequency is affected by many factors which include: temperature, light, age, size and stage of growth. Depending on your water source, the additives (mineral, carbon dioxide, and oxygen content) might vary substantially and affect the plant to a great extent. Water pH is a measure of growth. Depending on your water source, the additives (mineral, carbon dioxide, and oxygen content) might vary substantially and affect the plant to a great extent. Water pH is a measure of acid-alkalinity balance and is measured on a scale of 0-14, with 0 the most acid, 7 neutral, and 14 pure alkali. Every point increase or decrease on the pH scale reflects a 10-fold change in acidity or alkalinity. Most nutrients that plants use are soluble only in a limited range of acidity. Solubility also depends to some extent on the type of soil, planting mix, or hydroponic medium. If the water solution in the soil becomes too acid or alkaline, the nutrients dissolved in the water precipitate and become unavailable to the plants. When the seedlings suffer from moisture stress, the nutrients are locked up and plant growth is slowed. A conspicuous sign of water problems is the wilting of leaves. Also, an over-abundance of water can kill young marijuana plants and create a condition called damping off.

Nutrient Plants should be grown in a nutrient-rich medium with compost, manure and fertilizers when needed. The marijuana plant requires quite a number of essential nutrients to support all of its biochemical needs. Carbon, hydrogen and oxygen are three vital elements that are considered non-mineral element which allow plants to undergo photosynthesis. These three elements make up around 95% of the mass of the plant. Nitrogen, potassium, phosphorus, calcium, magnesium and sulphur are macro- nutrients needed by the plant in relatively large amounts.

Iron deficiency

Once the plant is in the ground or a container, the two easiest and most reliable ways to meet the plant's needs are to use a prepared hydroponic fertilizer, a liquid organic fertilizer, or compost teas. Fertilizers often contain a mixture of ingredients; hydroponic fertilizers are blended as balanced and complete nutrient formulas, non-hydroponic fertilizers often contain only macronutrients—nitrogen (N), phosphorus (P), and potassium (K).

Organic fertilizers, such as fish emulsion, guanos and manures, and many blends of organics, contain additional trace elements found in the organic matter from which they are developed. However, demand for critical nutrients, such as nitrogen (N), phosphorus (P), and potassium (K) changes with the growing conditions and stages during the plant's life cycle. During the vegetative stage (before flowering), marijuana uses more N than P and K. The plant's use of P increases when it begins to flower, while the need for K increases after fertilization to aid flower formation and seed production. Importantly, marijuana planters need to inspect their plants carefully to accurately diagnose any nutritional problem plaguing it. Throughout the plant's life stages, it is critical to keep a close eye on the plants for minor symptoms of deficiencies.

Temperature

Marijuana grows well in moderate temperatures – between 70° and 85°F (21°-29° C). When temperatures fall below 60°F, a plant's metabolic rate and photosynthesis slows while below 45°F, plants will experience tissue damage. Marijuana plants are very resilient and will survive outdoors over a wide range of temperatures, even including extremely hot weather, up to 120° F (29° C). However as the temperature fluctuates from the high 70s into the low 80s (20-25° C), plants use up more energy staying cool and maintaining faster cell metabolism. Besides, the air temperature, root temperature is just as important as the canopy temperature. When a plant's roots are kept warm, the rest of the plant can be kept cooler with no damage. Cold floors or earth slow germination and growth, it also encourages more of the plants to develop as males. Additionally, water temperature should be adjusted to balance out the air temperature. If the air is warm (over 75°F, 22°C) the water should be no more than 70°F (20°C). If the air is over 90°F (30°C) the water can be lowered from 70°F to 65° (from 20°C to 18°C).

Both high and low temperatures slow marijuana's rate of metabolism and growth. That is, low temperatures delay germination while high temperatures upset seed germination hereby causing poor germination. Also, strong light and low temperatures slow growth and decrease stem elongation. Contrariwise, when plants are given high temperatures and only moderate light, the stems elongate. However, different marijuana strains differ in their temperature inclinations by a few degrees, so some experimentation is usually required to find the ideal temperatures for the strain you are growing. It is essential for gardeners to understand that regulating temperature will also optimize harvest.

MARIJUANA VEGETATIVE PHASE

The vegetative stage is the stage where the marijuana plant shows the first sign of life. At this phase, plant continues to grow vegetatively — that is, it grows a main stem, branches and leaves (without any buds) but no flowers—until it receives environmental cues such as light. That is, shortening light periods prompt it to respond by beginning to flower. The cannabis plant only grows stems and leaves and is sturdy and resilient to challenges, it actually grows like a weed. The plant's development is very visible at this stage as the growth accelerates and it can grow as much as three inches in just one day. At this stage, the difference between cannabis varieties becomes quite noticeable. Unhampered vegetative growth is essential for a robust harvest as the plant's nutrient and water intake changes during the vegetative stage. The marijuana plant carries out transpiration at a more rapid rate and requires more water and higher levels of trace nutrients. Also, when grown indoors the lighting remains a vital component for growth. The duration of the vegetation stage varies greatly from one variety of marijuana to another. Additionally, it is important to avoid low humidity (below 40% RH) for vegetative marijuana plants as they prefer a comfortable room temperature or slightly warmer, around 70-85°F (20-30°C). Never allow plants to experience freezing temperatures in this stage. However, if everything is done right and the plant is growing in a healthy way it should gradually move to the next stage of growth within three to four weeks.

Auto-flowering cannabis varieties move automatically on to the flowering stage within two or three weeks. Regular or feminised varieties only start flowering once the days become shorter (outdoor cultivation) or the grower reduces the lighting period to 12 hours (indoor cultivation). However, indoor growers can keep the marijuana plants in the vegetative stage for as long or short as they want by providing at least 18 hours of light a day. This is usually accomplished by putting grow lights on a timer. Unlike outdoor growers who are overly reliant on the sun cycles to get plants to start making buds, indoor growers have more control over the final size and shape of their plant. A light period that keeps on for 17+ hours each day will deceive the marijuana, making it think that it is summer/grow time. Hence, as long as the marijuana plants get 17+ hours of light a day, they will remain in the vegetative stage, growing only stems and leaves.

MARIJUANA PRE- FLOWERING PHASE

This stage is typically referred to as 'the stretch'. It could take anything from one day to two weeks. Pre-flowers will begin to show around the fourth week into the vegetative growth depending on the strain in marijuana horticulture. The plant development occurs spectacularly with the plant almost doubling in size. Production of more branches and nodes occurs during this stage as the structure and foundation for flowering develops. The plant starts to develop bracts/bracteoles where

the branches meet the stem nodes. Also, it is essential to ensure that the plant has well-balanced nutrients during this phase as this will determine the quality of the overall harvest.

Female marijuana plant

Male marijuana plant

An undeniably important element of the pre-flowering phase is that the sex of the plant is able to be determined here. Usually, marijuana plants are either all male or all female and each sex has its own distinct flowers. The male marijuana plant will develop tiny, smooth, egg-shaped pollen sacks while the female plant will develop small V-shaped white or pink hairs called pistils. Growers remove and destroy the males because they have low levels of cannabinoids while female plants are cultivated for their high cannabinoid content. In the vegetative stage, it is important to prune the lower leaves of the plant to provide airflow under the canopy and to create cuttings for cloning. This also maximizes yield by forcing the plant's growth energy to the top limbs where they receive the most light.

MARIJUANA FLOWERING PHASE

The flowering or bloom period is the stage when the marijuana plants begin to produce aromatic flowers which with proper care will later be harvested, dried, cured and smoked. Hence, this is a particularly important stage in the plant's life cycle. Marijuana is a short-day plant. Therefore, as the days get shorter, marijuana determines when to flower based on the number of hours it receives of uninterrupted darkness. In order to flower correctly, marijuana plants need about twelve interrupted hours of darkness. However, the number of hours of darkness marijuana plants need to initiate flowering differs by variety. Sativas require a longer period of darkness than indicas because they developed near the equator, where the length of daylight is much more consistent than at northern latitudes, where indicas developed. Some sativas continue to grow vegetatively with 10 or 11 hours of darkness, which usually cues most plants to flower. When left unpollinated, female flowers develop without seeds, called *sin semilla* (which translates to "without seeds" in Spanish). Marijuana users prize seedless female flowers, known as sinsemilla because they produce far more useable buds than seeded buds; nothing is wasted on seed production. It is also important to medical users to minimize the amount of cannabis they must consume to be afforded relief. Otherwise when a female plant is fertilized with male pollen, the female flower buds will begin to develop seeds.

In natural growing environment outdoors, the plants photosynthesize during the day, turning light into energy and releasing oxygen while in darkness they begin to produce a hormone called florigen which is in charge of starting the flowering period. It measures the length of the dark period using the hormone phytochrome, which has two states, the inactive state, 'Pfr', occurs when it absorbs red spectrum of light at 666 nanometers. It also has a slight sensitivity to blue light. The hormone changes to its active form, 'Pr', over a period of two hours when the plant is in darkness. Hence, when the 'Pr' flowering hormone levels remain high for a critical period of time over several days, the plant changes from vegetative growth and initiates flowering. However, when growing marijuana indoors the flowering time of female marijuana plants is regulated by the length of the uninterrupted dark period, so gardens under lights can be forced to flower at any time with a timer switch. The gardener controls flowering time by regulating the light cycle. To induce flowering, the lights must be turned on and off with consistent regularity and the darkness must be uninterrupted. For that reason, it is essential to use a timer to regulate the lights. This is because variations in the lighting routines can easily stress the marijuana plants out and they might end up revegging which means they revert to the growth period.

The entire flowering phase lasts about seven to nine weeks and consists of these stages; transition, first buds, growth of buds, ripening of buds and harvest. The first one to three weeks are a transition phase and the plants are still growing rapidly, some strains double in height during this time. The reason for this major spurt of growth is so that the plant has ample size and strength to support the coming buds. Then in the third or fourth week, the first buds start to show on the plant instead of hairy pistils. At this phase of flowering where the plant is starting to spend more energy on growing flowers, it is important to feed it proper nutrients in appropriate dosages. At this point, the buds begin to thicken or fatten up and white pistils will be obvious on the plant. As this portion of the flowering stage progresses, the majority of the pistils remain white, signifying that the buds are getting denser and bigger every day. At this point, vegetative growth has ended and the plants concentrate more of their energy into flowering. The plant will have a very noticeable intensive odour as the plants start to produce capitate trichomes.

As at the sixth or seventh week, flower growth might continue in varieties that take longer to mature but any vegetative has completely stopped by this point. This is why it is important not to provide any nutrients that promote vegetative growth. Flower growth slows and then stops in seven-week varieties as the buds begin to ripen. The calyx behind the stigmas begins to swell and the odours of the seven-week varieties intensify. The calyxes in the seven-week varieties swell to near bursting as THC is produced in the glands and at the end of the week they will be ready. The trichomes stand more erect and the caps swell with newly produced resin. At the end of the week the flowers reach the peak zone. The odour is intense and the glands, filled with resin, fluoresce. Growth stops in the eight-week varieties as the flowers start to mature. Near the end of flowering the pistils on most strains will change from white to orange. It is a signal that new buds are not being produced anymore and harvest time is likely close. The exact week for harvest of marijuana is highly dependent on the strain being cultivated. After which the trichomes of the marijuana plant will turn from clear to milky as they increase in THC. The harvest window is typically around a week long, after which the THC will start degrading into CBN which is less potent and produces a sleepy feeling.

Auto-Flowering Plants

This peculiarity has been bred into several varieties that are available commercially as "auto-flowering" plants. These strains have developed their own automatic flowering system which means that no matter what light regime the marijuana plants are growing under, they will germinate, grow and flower in a predetermined pattern. Auto-flowering plants do not flower based on the quantity of light or darkness they are exposed to because they have adapted and survived in colder areas so they flower when they reach a particular size. Instead, auto-flowering plants begin to bloom depending on the amount of time they have been growing for. They can finish their full cycle from germination to harvest in just 80-90 days although some might take longer. These varieties make small plants for the most part.

MARIJUANA HARVESTING

The marijuana plant is ready to harvest when the bud ripens, pistils turn amber and the trichomes are no longer translucent. This colour change can be monitored under a microscope or hand lens. Typically, indica plants will be ready for harvest in approximately 50 to 60 days. So for most indicas grown indoors, the window of harvest is about two weeks long for various strains. Sativa plants can stay in bloom longer, ranging between 60 to 70 days. There is more than one way to harvest the plant. The methods fall into two key types: harvesting the entire plant – this method of harvest is quicker, easier and requires less monitoring of individual bud maturity or harvesting individual buds as they ripen- removing the most ripe buds first.

Marijuana buds being harvested

The advantage of harvesting individual buds as they ripen is that it gives the lower buds and buds hidden inside the canopy the chance to fully mature. Outdoors, buds may be hidden by fan leaves or other plant parts. The variety is a factor in how the plants mature. Some plants ripen top first, others ripen bottom up, and usually buds closest to the outer edge ripen first. Waiting the extra time and picking no bud before it is ripe assures the finest harvest.

In general, harvesting involves manicuring, drying and curing. Manicuring is the process of removing the leaves that are growing around the buds. There are four steps to trimming ripe marijuana: clipping the stem from the plant, clipping the buds from the stem, removing the large leaves and removing the small leaves from the bud. Curing is an oxidation and polymerization process before drying during which many of the cell's metabolic processes continue for a little longer. Buds continue to cure when they are kept at about 60-70° F (15-21° C) with humidity of 50%. After the buds are cured, they are dried at 50% humidity and the buds dry gradually over a week or two, depending on their size. The length of the drying process is affected by bud size, size of the drying space as compared with the amount of bud drying, temperature and humidity. During drying, the plants can then be hung upside down on hooks or wires that are attached securely to the walls.

Usually the dried buds are stored in an airtight non-plastic container and stored in a cool, dark place. The containers are burped several times a day (by removing the lid to the container for a short period of time). This allows for air exchange and removes any remaining moisture. Different strains many cure at different rates. Buds that are cured properly and dried slowly have the smooth draw of fine herb.

CHAPTER 2: INDOOR AND OUTDOOR MARIJUANA CULTIVATION

Marijuana is one of many plants that can be grown indoors, outdoors or in a combination of both locations. This adaptation is due to the extensive amount of work put into adapting and domesticating cannabis hybrids. However, marijuana growers need to consider a number of factors to determine the most appropriate and comfortable location for them to grow their plants. For example, if indoors, is there enough space for the plants to thrive? The number of plants to be grown? Preparedness for all the vagaries of being a grower and so on. If outdoors, is there a concealed location? How is the weather where you live? How is the soil? Is the season appropriate? The environment in which the marijuana plant is grown is one of the most important factors affecting the quality and yield of the harvest.

Marijuana has long been cultivated outdoors and is one of the oldest crops in existence. Growing marijuana indoors, however, came to be less than a century ago. Prohibition of marijuana around the world was the origin of indoor cultivation. Growing a crop without natural sunlight might seem disadvantageous but technological advancements have the plants achieving exceptional aesthetic quality and flavour with higher THC percentages.

INDOOR MARIJUANA CULTIVATION

Indoor cultivation of marijuana provides several benefits including control, reproducibility and risk mitigation. All these are achieved through precise lighting, temperature, humidity, carbon dioxide content and controlled air movement within the indoor growing space. Indoor cultivation also allows growers to achieve a more reproducible product and multiple harvests, per year. However, cultivating marijuana indoors is more complicated and expensive than growing outdoors but it allows the grower complete control over the growing environment. Though it is safe to say the cost to grow indoors mirrors the reward.

Indoor

plants grown under bright lights

Marijuana can be grown indoors in a soil or soil-like medium with lighting (natural or artificial), fertilizers, watering and airflow. Hence, growers employ the use of equipments to help create a stable environment that mimics the necessary periods of light and darkness to grow the plants through the flowering phase. This includes horticultural lighting, fans to create a gentle breeze, dehumidifiers to maintain the proper humidity, HVAC (heating, ventilation, proper humidity, and air conditioning). Indoor marijuana can be cultivated in a closet, garage, cabinet, spare room or a basement. A relatively new indoor growing method involves the use of a grow tent. These are plastic or metal framed tent which are covered in a strong, reflective plastic and have light proof zipper doors. Tents come in different sizes and many already have holes for exhaust fans as well as mounts for lighting. Hence, it is important to properly plan, design and implement the indoor garden to ensure a healthy and bountiful harvest. The grower should consider; the height of ceiling, how much insulation the space offers and ease of access to electricity and water.

Lighting

Lights often represent the lifeblood of plants grown indoors as the quality of lights will be the fundamental environmental factor in the quantity and quality of yield. Because any sunlight that they might receive is sparse, artificial light is valuable and necessary. Plants need the light to perform photosynthesis, which is vital for sugar and tissue production. During the vegetative phase, plants need a minimum of sixteen hours of light. The most common schedule for growers during this phase is eighteen hours of light and six hours of darkness. To initiate flowering plants need a shorter day, with twelve hours of light and twelve hours of darkness. Indoor lights produce bigger flowers (more buds) than natural window lighting. This means growers will get more THC quality with artificial lights than natural sunlight indoors. Whether the breeder is growing the plants in a room, attic or basement, must assess the viability, both in terms of space and electrical capacity, of bringing in a large amount of lights. Low levels of light slow photosynthesis, delay growth and results in a poor harvest. Also, if the lights are too far away, the plants will not enjoy enough of it and will grow spindly. If the lights are too close, it can damage the plants and ruin the colas.

High-Intensity Discharge (HID) Lighting

Most plants grow under most light spectra but prefer a full spectrum light. However, certain plants like marijuana can be grown successfully using both high pressure sodium (HPS) and metal halide (MH) lamps. MH lights are a type of high-intensity discharge (HID) lights that work by igniting gas in a tube with a spark of electricity. MH which produces a blue-ish white light is used for the vegetative phase of growth as it encourages short inter-nodes and inhibits cell elongation, creating a shorter/stockier plant. These lamps also produce more ultraviolet radiation than high pressure sodium lamps which may play a role in the flowering (and for marijuana, the amount of THC).

However, the crisp white light emitted by standard MH lamps is low in the red spectrum. Since plants need red spectrum light for photosynthesis and flowering, its absence is felt. Nonetheless, under metal halides, plants grow quickly and flowering is profuse, with heavier budding than under fluorescents. Also, the brighter light penetrates a bit deeper into the canopy. High pressure sodium (HPS) bulbs which produce light that is on the red-orange end of the spectrum. They are highly efficient HID lights that produce a very effective spectrum of light to promote growth during the flowering phase. HPS triggers a greater flowering response in plants and are thus used for the second (reproductive) phase of growth or by people who wish to utilize a single type of lighting because they need no supplemental lighting during any stage of growth. Most HPS bulbs are double-ended and can last 10,000 hours without losing efficiency; they however produce a significant amount of heat thereby increasing air-conditioning requirements. They produce about 15% more light than MH and use the same configuration: lamp, reflector, and remote ballast. The 600- and 750w HPS lamps are about 7% more efficient than the other sizes

High Pressure Sodium (HPS) Lamps

In addition to bulbs, HID lighting setups require a ballast and hood/reflector for each light. Some ballasts are designed for use with either MH or HPS lamps while some run both. The ballast converts house current to the appropriate voltage. Ballasts used to power garden lights are usually remote from the light, connected by a long electrical cord.

The convenience of this is that the heavy ballasts are not hanging from the ceiling, only the much lighter and less cumbersome reflector and bulb are stationed above the plant canopy. Magnetic ballasts are cheaper than digital ballasts but run hotter and are less efficient. Generally, digital ballasts are a better option but they are more expensive. Digital ballasts have many advantages over magnetic ballasts, they are quieter and more efficient and operate at a higher frequency, minimizing the wear and increasing lamp life. It is important for growers to buy digital ballasts that are of good quality because bad ballasts are often not well-shielded and can create electromagnetic interference that will affect radio and Wi-Fi signals.

Light-Emitting Diodes (LED) Lights

Light-emitting diodes (LED) lights are another form of high-intensity lighting that has been growing in popularity as their technology advanced. LEDs come in many configurations, including flood lights, panels, bars, circles, and rectangular fixtures. LED lights produce a spectrum suited for all phases of plant life and so they make great lamps for closet cultivation or other spaces where height is an issue. They typically cost more than other grow lights but they last much longer, are more energy efficient and give off a lot less radiant heat than HID lighting. LED lamps emit virtually no heat, so they can be placed very close to the garden and are not encumbered with tubes for air or water cooling, heavy ventilation, or any of the other problems or inconveniences of HID lamps. They also have a long operating life; good safety characteristics and adjustable spectral quality that allow optimization to improve photosynthetic efficiency and plant form and function. The best LED designs generate a fuller spectrum of light which can lead to bigger yields and better quality. However, LED lights should be placed about 2-10 inches from the tops of the plants as if the leaves touch them, they will be burned.

Fluorescent Lighting

Another choice of lighting for growers is fluorescents. Fluorescents lights are affordable and use minimal wattage to produce a low-intensity light. They tend to be cheaper to set up as reflector, ballast and bulbs are included in a single package and they do not require a cooling system. Fluorescents come with various spectral outputs, which are determined by the type of phosphor used to coat the surface of the tube. Each phosphor type emits a different set of light colors, identified as "warm white," "cool white," and "daylight" or "natural white." These names signify the kind of light the tube produces, with daylight or natural white coming closest to approximating the sun's spectrum. They are available in strips or larger arrays of multiple bulbs and are commonly used during germination and propagation of seeds and clones. They however cannot be used during the flowering phase. Space is another concern with fluorescents as it would require nineteen 4-foot long T5 HO bulbs to equal the output of a single 600 watt HPS bulb.

Creating the Ideal Growing Environment Indoors

When cultivating marijuana indoors, the cultivator should endeavour to maintain as close to a perfect atmosphere inside the grow-room as possible. Generally, the grower has to ensure that the plant is provided with the optimal temperature, humidity, air circulation, carbon dioxide and nutrients.

Temperature and Humidity

The atmospheric temperature should be regulated and maintained within a specific range. As such the grower needs to monitor the grow room temperature using a thermometer or hygrometer. Young growing marijuana plants grow fastest under warmer temperature, in the 70-85°F (20-30°C) range. However when the plants are older, they thrive under cooler temperature, around 75

85°F (18-26°C) to produce buds with the best colour, trichomes production and smell. The right temperature range for the plants when the lights are on is between 70-85°F and between 58-70°F when the lights are off. In hot temperatures, marijuana plants can lose a considerable amount of moisture which can lead to stress. In contrast, very low temperatures can cause the plant to stop absorbing and circulating vital nutrients.

Furthermore, humidity control is essential when growing marijuana indoors as the plants benefit from different levels of humidity during the varying phase of their life cycle. For example, seedlings like high humidity levels of around 65-70%, around 55-60% during their vegetative phase. In the final weeks of vegetative growth, the humidity in the grow room should be around 40% where it should stay during flowering to avoid mold and mildew issue. The best way to control humidity in the grow room is with a dehumidifier/humidifier. Dehumidifiers work the same way as a refrigerator but instead of cooling a space, moisture in the air condenses and collects on the cold tubes.

Air circulation

Good air flow within the growing space is important to the plants' health. Plants depend on the air movement to grow strong and robustly. Also, because plants need fresh air to survive, it is important to always keep the windows open and let the grow room refresh itself. Most indoor growers will need a fan to vent out extra hot air from the grow lights. The size of the exhaust fan depends on the size of the grow space and amount of heat generated by the heating system. Alternatively, a sealed, artificial environment can be created by using an air conditioner, dehumidifier and supplemental CO_2 system; however, this is quite expensive. Vigorous air movement mimics natural outdoor environment so it is important to have a constant light breeze in the grow room as this strengthens the plants stems and creates a less hospitable environment for mold and flying pests. A wall-mounted circulating fan is appropriate for this purpose but it should not point directly at the plants as this can cause windburn.

Carbon Dioxide Supplementation Adequate levels of carbon dioxide are crucial to the process of photosynthesis and must be maintained for the plants to grow efficiently. When plants are growing in an enclosed area, there is a limited amount of CO_2 for them to use. Under bright lights, CO_2 is used up quickly. Enclosed gardens with no ventilation are also rapidly depleted to the point where the photosynthesis rate slows to a virtual stop at 200 ppm. Only when more CO_2 is added to the mix does photosynthesis resume. A closed closet or other small gardening space can be recharged with CO_2 simply by opening the door or curtain to let in fresh air. This increases the CO_2 content of the closet passively, as air naturally equalizes the concentrations of oxygen (O_2) and CO_2 inside and outside the growing space, exchanging the higher O_2 levels with CO_2. In the event of a lack of adequate levels of carbon dioxide, it can be increased by using bottled carbon dioxide, carbon dioxide tanks, carbon dioxide generators, a baking soda and vinegar mixture in a container or dry ice. However, the best way to do it is with a CO_2 generator. These generators will keep a steady flow of CO_2 coming into the room and the plants will be able to take it in adroitly. The amount of carbon dioxide in the room is directly proportional to how large the plant (and later the buds) will end up growing.

Germination Soil

Marijuana plants only grow as big and healthy as their growing medium lets them. Hence, when growing indoors it is important to use a top-shelf soil from the beginning as starting with the wrong soil can make the plants weak and sickly. Soil also contains beneficial microbes and nutrients that keep the plants healthy. Marijuana has a slightly different growing requirement than other plants. It thrives well in slightly acidic soil with a pH of roughly 6-6.8 (5.5-6.5 for soilless mediums). When choosing the right soil, it is important to consider how well it drains and retains water as the roots will have a hard time taking in oxygen when there is too much water. But at the same time, the soil should not be too loose that water easily runs through it, leaving little for the plant to use. The right pH value in the soil helps to absorb more nutrients therefore growers must be vigilant in regularly checking the pH levels to make sure the soil is conducive for the plants.

Water

Water is one of the basic needs of most plants. This is especially true in the case of marijuana as water plays quite a number of crucial roles in throughout the plants' life cycle. For example water is what gives the marijuana plant its vigour and flexibility while also regulating the plant's internal temperature. When growing marijuana indoors, water becomes the medium that carries nutrients. Unmodified water is used to flush hydroponic and soilless systems regularly. However, it is important to water properly as overwatering leads to roots choking due to the struggle to get oxygen. While with under-watering the plants become thirsty and unable to regulate their internal temperature. Also, some places have very hard water or tap water with undesirable impurities so growers in these areas will likely need to use purified water to get the best results. Typically, a plant growing in an acidic environment with a low pH is very small, often growing only a few inches (approx 7.5 cm) in several months. Plants growing in a high-pH environment look pale and sickly and also have stunted growth. Checking the pH, mineral or chemical content and the acidity or alkalinity of the water should be done regularly by the grower. Knowing these will determine the correct amount of nutrients to feed the plants or if fresh water needs to be introduced. Water that is too acidic can alternatively be neutralized using potassium bicarbonate, or wood ash. Water that is too alkaline can be adjusted using nitric acid, sulfuric acid, citric acid (Vitamin C), kombucha tea or vinegar.

Nutrients

Plants grown in a nutrient-rich medium with compost, manure, or time-release fertilizers may need no additional fertilizing when planted in a large enough container or outdoor garden. The quality/quantity of nutrients the marijuana plants have access to determines the grower's yield (plant's production of dense buds). A good friable soil mix is one that is rich with compost, living organisms, vitamins and minerals that can supply the plants with enough nutrients for their whole cycle. Marijuana needs three macronutrients to grow: nitrogen (N), phosphorus (P), potassium (K). Different nutrients formulas will carry these compounds in different concentrations. But beyond NPK fertilizer formulas, the plants also need micronutrients like calcium, sulphur, zinc, boron, manganese, copper and iron. A healthy combination of these nutrients will ensure a bountiful harvest. The lack of these elements slows down growth and makes the plant more susceptible to pests, molds and diseases. However, an excess can alter the pH level of the soil or cause nutrient build-up that prevents root absorption.

Plants container

The type of the container to be used is highly dependent on the medium, the system and the size of plants. In a broad sense, the size of the pot will determine the size of the plant. In general, five- gallon pots are a good size for small to medium plants. A flood and drain, tray-style hydroponic system may use small net pots filled with the chosen growth medium. While a soil grow may use ten-gallon nursery pots to grow a few large plants. Inexpensive options include disposable perforated plastic bags or cloth bags and five gallon buckets. There are also 'smart pots' that are designed to enhance airflow to the plant's root zone. Also, when growing marijuana plants in a container, you have to choose the right size of pot. Plants that get root-bound from being in a too-small container will grow more slowly and be prone to problems. For fastest growth rate, it is better to plant young seedlings in a very small container like a disposable cup. The reason why it is better to start with a small container is that marijuana plant's young root thrives on oxygen so when the grower waters the seedling in a very big container, the oxygen is used up quickly and the large size of the container will prevent the growing medium from drying out. Containers must be able to drain well so growers can adapt containers by creating drainage holes at the sides or bottom.

Pests

Even indoors, the marijuana plant can have a pest problem. Bugs do occur even where there is seemingly no way for them to get in. To combat this, a mild pesticide like Neem oil is needed to spray the plants from top to bottom while paying special attention to the leaves undersides. Warm, humid stagnant air provides an ideal environment for mold, mildew, fungi and certain pests. Pulling in cooler, drier air eliminates this problem and having adequate air circulation helps to discourage infestation of small flying insects such as gnats.

OUTDOOR MARIJUANA CULTIVATION

Outdoor marijuana cultivation is common in both rural and urban areas. It might be best to grow indica-based strains because of its heavy yields, quick maturing time and short stature. However, outdoor growing is also great for sativa because of its cerebral high, better response to sunlight and lower odour emissions. Growing outdoors has different challenges than growing indoors. For example, you cannot control light, temperature or humidity and it harder to control pests and weeds. Also, the grower has to worry about privacy, stealth, possible pollination and plant thieves.

However, with the right marijuana strain and a good environment, it costs significantly less to plant outdoors since the grower does not need to purchase grow lights or create an indoor grow area. Outdoor growing is the most natural way to grow as the sun provides most of the marijuana plant's lighting needs. Nonetheless the grower has to protect the plant against the elements; watering when it is dry/hot, preventing the plants from getting overwatered when it is too rainy and protecting the plants from extreme temperatures. Some ideal locations for an outdoor grow include; balcony, personal garden, roof terrace, a forest, an open field.

Plants can be grown directly in the ground, or in plant containers/pots. Another method is to start the plants in pots and then move them to the ground. Plants can be moved outdoors by 3-4 weeks after germination. However, if the growing pots are large enough, there might be no need to transplant. As long as the location provides maximum sunlight and the plants is not attacked by pests, a potted plants with at least a foot of growing room in all directions will be grown to fruition. Also, potted plants are convenient as they can be moved around to maximize sunlight or protect them from harsh conditions such as rain, heavy winds or extreme temperatures.

While growing outdoors, it is important for the grower to consider the proximity of the growing area to the caretaker. If the plants are easily accessible then the grower can be more flexible in terms of watering and feeding the garden. However if the plants are a considerable distance away, the grower needs to explore the options of a grow medium that can hold moisture for an extended period of time.

In the northern hemisphere, marijuana can be planted in early to mid-spring and usually harvested in mid-fall. In the southern hemisphere, the growing season will be reversed, planting in the fall and harvesting in spring. During the first half of the season, the daytime period increases until the summer solstice which occurs in the northern hemisphere on or around June 21 and in the southern hemisphere on or around December 21. While the daylight hours increase, the plant's vegetative stage takes place. During the vegetation, the plants will develop the roots and the stems that will serve as the foundation for growth until flowering. After the solstice, the available daylight hours decrease allowing the plant to naturally transition into the flowering period. It is important for growers to plan their planting schedule to ensure the plants are able to finish their flowering before the cold, rainy weather is able to distress them.

Seeds or clones

There are two ways to begin a marijuana grow. One is to obtain seeds and germinate them in a growing medium. Growing from seed ensures a genetically

unique specimen that will feature traits from both the male and female cultivars used to create the strain. The strain may be heirloom meaning both the male and female were of the same strain or a hybrid meaning two different strains were bred together to create a novel strain. One potential downside of using seeds is that the grower could end up with more male plants. A way round this is using feminized seeds which have a much higher chance of producing female plants.

A second option is to start a grow from clones although this is preferred by indoor growers. A clone is a cutting from a cannabis plant that when rooted produces a genetically identical copy of the mother plants. This can be beneficial as it allows growers to replicate desirable traits. However, it will also pass down negative traits such as disease. Also, cloned plants never develop the thick central taproot that goes into the ground which stabilizes the plant and consumes groundwater. As a result, they produce lesser yields and are vulnerable to drought and windy conditions.

Sunlight

The sun is the best light for growing as it offers a full spectrum which allows marijuana to thrive. Each part of the light spectrum contributes to the growth and development of the molecules that make up the resulting plant including terpenes and cannabinoids. The sun requires no expense, no electricity, and its bright beams do not draw suspicion. During the summer, the sun is brighter than artificial lighting and is self-regulating. When growing with the sun, the grower needs to ensure the marijuana plants get at least eight hours of direct sunlight each day. The marijuana plant has very high light needs; hence, it is essential for it get enough light at every phase in its life cycle. In the northern hemisphere, the outdoor garden has more southern exposure which means that the garden is open mostly to the south, facing the sun's archway throughout the day. On the other hand, in the southern hemisphere, northern exposure is preferred due to the sun's position in the sky relative to the earth's axis. Of course, for growers planting close to the equator, this is less of a concern as the sun's arc will pass directly overhead. Marijuana grows fast when the daylight starts to increase during spring on to summer. The plant will continue to grow vegetatively while there is over twelve hours of daylight.

Watering

A common mistake when growing outdoors is overwatering. The plants should be given just as much water they can make use of when the soil has dried up. However, watering and adding needed nutrients to the soil is important. Wilting plants and dry soil are a direct sign that the plants need water. A good rule of thumb is that a large plant needs ten gallons of water a day. When growing in a dry and hot climate, a grower can dig beneath the plants before adding rocks or clay-rich soil underneath the planting holes as a means of slowing drainage. On the other hand, growers who plant in wet climates need to improve drainage as marijuana that grows in a waterlogged soil is susceptible to root diseases. Soil drainage can be improved in the following ways; planting the marijuana in beds or raised mounds, digging ditches to ensure that water flows away from the plants and adding pebbles, perlite or gravel to the soil.

Pests and weed control

Young marijuana plants outdoors might be eaten and damaged by snails, kangaroos and other animals. Caterpillars, moles and beetles are some of the most common pests for outdoor growers. They eat leaves and sometimes tunnel through the middle of plant buds. Hence, growers must examine their plants regularly and can use wire cages to keep the animals at bay. Another method of fighting pests is to grow companion plants. Companion plants are plants of a different species (like clover, rosemary, basil and marigold) to marijuana that are planted near cannabis to repel pests.

As the plants start to germinate, it is important to keep the area free from weeds. Avoid using any weed killers like that might also affect the marijuana plants. It should be noted that weeds will end up taking a lot of the water and nutrients meant for plants and reduce the quality of the yield if they are not stamped out quickly. But the best way to get rid of weeds is simply by pulling them by hand. Also, a light layer of mulch on top of the soil might prevent additional weeds from sprouting in the middle of the cycle.

Remove the males

Cannabis is one of the many species in the plant kingdom that produce male and female flowers on separate plants. In order for female flowers to ripen without seeds, they must remain unpollinated (unfertilized). Female plants produce flower buds rich in psychoactive compounds while males produce spindly flowers. Male marijuana plants should be removed to prevent them from pollinating the females. Once the females are pollinated, they divert energy meant for producing buds into the development of seeds; therefore reducing the impending harvest. Also, males have a lower level of THC than females. This culling should be done early in the male plants' development, before any large flower clusters appear. Even a single open flower can release enough pollen to fertilize dozens of neighboring female buds.

Pruning

Depending on the variety, outdoor plants can grow up to twelve feet or more in height. Pruning is the process of selectively trimming the plants so that they produce more flowers or buds. Pruning is sometimes needed to keep marijuana plants at a manageable size and for more yields. When the main stem is cut, the lower branches increase in size and the plants grow other strong branches. When these are pruned, the plant becomes bushier and less taller. Plant with the main stem clipped will most likely produce greater yield than unclipped. Pruning should be done during the plant's vegetative stage. While pruning has beneficial effects to growing marijuana plants, it can also cause dangerous levels of stress with a hormonal release. In this case, the response includes the release of jasmonic acid, a growth inhibitor which makes the plants stop growing and focus on healing. This is the reason why over-pruning can lead to stunted growth and should be conducted with great care.

Guerrilla cultivation

This is an option that growers who do not have a garden for outdoor growing and opportunity to grow indoors usually use. These growers find a suitable piece of land be it in a forest, woods or scrublands where plants can be left to fend for

themselves till harvest time. Basically, guerrilla farming is growing away from a property that is yours that is, in public areas or on another person's property. However, it is important that this location has a suitable soil and good supply of water. In some cases an irrigation system might be needed. Guerrilla farming is hard work and most often is prone to thieves and rip-offs.

Greenhouses

In recent years, consumers have started to clamour that products across all markets be sustainable. Consumers want non-genetically modified products, bred free of pesticides and produced in a way that does not negatively impact the environment. Cannabis breeders are not left out of these responsibilities. Hence, advancements in growing techniques keep the health of the consumer and the environment at the foreground of the marijuana industry. Greenhouse operations have become a popular choice, presenting the positives of both outdoor and indoor setups. Greenhouses have created a union of the sun with the protection of an indoor facility. They offer the sustainable environmental-friendly alternative that consumers are interested in. Greenhouses strike a balance between the indoor and outdoor cultivation. It does not include the tricky complexities of indoor grow room set-up and it is more consistent, secure and predictable than growing outdoors. They also provide ample protection from the elements and use fewer resources than an indoor grow. Growers are also less likely to encounter pests like deer, rabbits, pests and birds when growing in a greenhouse. Through solar radiation, the sun warms up the soil and the plants within the greenhouse. The plants in turn release energy known as infrared radiation. As a result, energy trapped within the greenhouse maintains the warm environment needed for growing.

This technique allows for year-round cultivation, climate control and a controlled exposure to sunlight. Greenhouses also offer growers the ability to control the hours of sunlight the plants receive (much like turning the light on and off in an indoor garden) by covering the greenhouse with a black tarp that deprives the plants of sunlight. Greenhouse cultivation can be either hydroponic or utilize compost in containers. Greenhouse structures range from inexpensive polyvinyl chloride (PVC) tubes often called "hoop houses" to highly-engineered, fully automated and purpose-built steel structures. Due to their efficiency, greenhouses are quickly becoming highly preferred amongst large-scale cultivators.

INDOOR VS. OUTDOOR MARIJUANA CULTIVATION

Environmental-friendliness

With the popularity of indoor growing comes the excessive consumption of energy because grow rooms require lights, ventilation systems and other equipments that use a lot of electricity. It is estimated that growing marijuana indoors uses the equivalent of 200 pounds of coal to grow just a single pound of bud. In contrast, outdoor growing needs only the sun, air and water to thrive. It does not produce any carbon footprint; in fact it contributes to the dynamics of the ecosystem.

Controlled vs. Natural Climates

Controlling the temperature, light source, C02 production and humidity creates a stable habitat for the plants' growth without having to risk outdoor elements. On the other hand, no bulb can produce the same spectrum of light unique to the sun. This, in turn, limits indoor gardens to smaller yields and less vigorous plants.

Quality of buds

The blend of the sun, natural soil and fresh air often gives the outdoor marijuana a distinct flavour. However, unlike the protected indoor crops, elements such as snow, frost, rain, hail and gusts of wind might cause damage. For this reason, the final product might look a bit worse for wear compared to buds grown indoors. The indoor grower typically finds cosmetically pristine flowers with higher THC percentages. Being able to control the environment and expedite breeding has resulted in aesthetically beautiful strains with magnificent flavour profiles. Introducing higher CO_2 levels than in the natural environment increases bud growth and produces THC levels that are difficult to obtain outdoors

Effort and Price

Both indoor and outdoor grows demand substantial upfront costs but the difference becomes apparent in the long-term. Planting outdoors does not require the expenses that indoor growing does. The plants mostly get water, lights, air, and carbon dioxide for free. Exorbitant amount of money are spent to control the climate for indoor growing, increasingly so with the continuous turnover involved in indoor garden. Hence, pruning, trellising, watering, feeding and harvest work are ongoing and more demanding for indoor gardens and smaller yields. Outdoors, the grower is working on just one crop throughout the season and will not need as much labour. The high costs of indoor farming may be recouped through breeding projects, year-round harvests and potent products that have higher selling points. However, with the rising cost of energy and an increasing demand for more flowers in the marketplace, outdoor growing may be able to supply the market with quality products at a more reasonable price. For instance it is quite common for outdoor marijuana plants to grow nearly six feet tall and plants of this size offer up to 500 grams of dried bud.

CHAPTER 3: HYDROPONIC GARDENING

Hydroponic gardening is a term for growing of plants in a soilless nutrient solution, with or without an inert medium to provide physical root support. Indoor growers are increasingly turning to soilless, hydroponic media for cultivating marijuana plants. Put simply, hydroponic marijuana refers to plants grown using a nutrient-rich solution and an inert growing medium rather than nutrient-rich soil. It is a lot neater than growing with soil, less likely to attract pests and its nutrient problems are fixed faster and easier. This method requires feeding with concentrated solutions of mineral salt that are absorbed directly by the roots through the process of osmosis. In general, it consists of a non-soil media medium exposed to a nutrient and water flow. Media such as fused basalt rock and chalk (Rockwool), coconut fiber (coco coir), vermiculite and clay pellets (hydroton) can significantly improve nutrient delivery. These soilless mixes are widely available and can even be combined to create an optimized growing medium. Soilless media can be used in automated hydroponic setups or in hand-watered individual containers. With the plant's root exposed, hydroponically grown marijuana can grow faster and more efficiently, requiring less water and fewer nutrients but also requiring monitoring systems to ensure a stable pH.

Hydroponic plants need a stable pH to survive so growers need to test the pH of the water to ensure an optimal growing environment. Nutrients are more available to the plants when the environment is acidic therefore a pH of 5.5-5.8 is necessary. Therefore, growers can use a pH testing kit to take regular readings and change the nutrient solution weekly to main this pH range. Clearly, this hydroponics is meant for quicker nutrient uptake leading to faster growth and greater yields. However, it requires a higher level of attention as plants are more sensitive to over/underfeeding, nutrient lockout and burn. Growers must be selective about marijuana strains to grow hydroponically. Sativas grow into towering, large plants hence they might not be the best choice especially since plants grown within these systems grow rapidly and explosively. Smaller, more compact strains are best for indoor hydroponic systems because it allows the grower to cultivate several plants within a smaller space.

GROWING MEDIUM

Growers need to select an inert growing medium, that is, a substance that will hold in place the intersection of the stem and roots. It is from this location the roots will grow down in search of water and nutrients. The medium hereby allows the plant's roots to be well oxygenated. Each medium has its own unique benefits and peculiarities and some are more efficient with particular systems.

Rockwool

Rockwool also known as mineral wool is one of the most common forms of hydroponic media for very young plants. It is made by heating rock and chalk to 3000°F and air is blown through the mixture to create thin fibers of rocky materials. It is an inert substance and its composition of mineral or rock fibers provides sterile environment with a unique capacity to hold water and resistance to mold. It is also inexpensive and easily accessible. Rockwool has a tremendous ability to retain water which allows for good hydration of the upper root system. Rockwool is constructed so that 18% of the space is reserved for air, even after the blocks have been irrigated to saturation. Water tension does not rise as the material becomes drier, so it is easy for the plant to absorb moisture until it is used up. These two characteristics mean that rockwool retains both water and air, so the roots' needs for oxygen and water are easily met.

**Young roots growing out of a Rockwool cube**

But it also means that the overabundance of water might cause a fungus problem and a lack of oxygen in the plant's roots. However, it quickly exposes any watering or feeding lapses and skipping a day of watering could be detrimental when using it, especially for young plants. Additionally, rockwool has a high pH that could be detrimental to marijuana so it must be thoroughly rinsed and treated to a pH of 5.5-6 before use. Growers need to be careful when working with rockwool because its dust and fibers pose health risks. They can cause skin rash or lodge in your lungs, causing temporary micro-ulcers.

Coco coir

Coco coir is the fibrous material found on and in coconut shells. Horticultural coir is made from ripe coconuts. As the fruit ripens the fibers, initially composed mostly of cellulose, change to high lignin content. It is favoured by growers because it is a renewable and sustainable medium. Coco coir provides the ease of soil gardening with the rapid growth of hydroponics by using fibrous coconut husks instead of a potting mix. Coco coir is an inert medium with a neutral pH that does not provide or maintain any nutrient for the plant. However, compared to just soil growing, it absorbs moisture much easier, allowing plants to take up more nutrients and retain oxygen more efficiently because of its lighter texture. The fibers not only absorb water but also chemically hold nutrients and buffer nutrient swings. Coconut fibres are also known to protect roots from infection due to the plant-stimulating hormones. They are also resistant to fungal and bacterial growth. These qualities are great for growers that know how to appropriately adjust pH allowing for quick pH and nutrients changes. However, in the case of human error such as adding too much nutrients, it provides a more forgiving buffer by reducing shock stress. It can be used by itself or added to soil or hydroton for improved drainage and growth capability.

Marijuana plants growing in Coco Coir

There are various ways in which coco coir can be watered. The flood and drain hydroponic system in which the nutrient system, controlled by a pump and timer, temporarily floods from beneath the plant instead of dripping from above like most systems. Coco is much easier for growers to flush than DWC because the entire reservoir does not need to be changed. Also, it is important to use calcium and magnesium in the coco growing medium as the combination of these nutrients helps to keep the plant healthy. Calcium helps in rapid root development, nutrient uptake and protein synthesis. Magnesium is an important component in chlorophyll production that helps plants with photosynthesis as well as synthesizing sugars and protein.

Perlite

Perlite is a volcanic glass that expands when exposed to high temperatures. It usually looks like small white pebbles but does not weigh much. It is sterile, inert and has a neutral pH. The hard pieces remain stable for years. They wick water through capillary action. While it can be done, cannabis is not just grown in just perlite. The surface of each perlite particle is covered with tiny cavities hence it highly permeable but it also holds nutrients and moisture relatively. This means it will help prevent compaction and allow nutrients and water to circulate easily which is an important aspect of plant's growth. Perlite's bright white color protects seeds by keeping them cool and moist even when placed under bright sunlight. It reflects light back to plant foliage which further enhances growth. Because perlite cannot hold onto much water, many growers mix it with their soilless medium or soil to improve air and drainage.

Vermiculite

This is another crushed volcanic rock like perlite. Vermiculite rock is mined and then exfoliated by heating it to 1650-2010°F (900-1100°C), this process also sterilizes it. It absorbs and holds water, buffers nutrients, and provides space for oxygen to get to the roots. Vermiculite also has traces of minerals like silicon, magnesium, aluminum and phosphorus. Aside from holding nutrients it slowly breaks up as it releases its magnesium and iron atoms. By interacting with the water/nutrient solution and providing a convenient space for colonization, the medium promotes thriving rhizosphere activity. Although it has great drainage properties, growers usually elect to mix it with other medium because it tends to disintegrate after a long period of use. Vermiculite contains virtually no nutrients so it is an excellent planting medium ingredient for hydroponics. It is usually mixed with perlite or wood chips. Vermiculite can become waterlogged when used on its own but is ideal for germinating seeds. However, certain types of vermiculite should be avoided because it contains toxins that harm the plant.

Hyrdroton or Clay pebbles

Hydroton systems can be blended with soil or other soilless medium or used alone in a hydroponic system. It is a lightweight expanded clay aggregate composed of porous clay pebbles but it does not retain water like rockwool or coco coir does. Due to its size, it wicks moisture up to the roots and enables oxygen to flow. It also dries out very quickly so it needs to be kept hydrated especially when used solely. Clay pebbles are porous, lightweight and pH-neutral and can be used in active hydroponic setups but are not good at lifting nutrients from reservoirs in passive systems. It is cost effective because it can be reused indefinitely and makes a useful medium to mix with coconut fiber.

AEROPONICS

Aeroponics are hydroponic systems in which the roots are suspended in the air and lightly sprayed with a nutrient solution intermittently. Aeroponics systems are used mostly for cloning. This method is most usually executed without a growing medium, although a small amount may be used to the seed or root a clone. Aeroponics systems recurrently spray roots floating in the air. Plants sit in a tray above a water/nutrient reservoir with their roots dangling down. Solution from the reservoir is sprayed up onto the roots at regular intervals and excess solution drips down into the reservoir. The mid-air feeding allows the roots to absorb much needed oxygen, thereby increasing metabolism and growth rate while slowing down water loss due to evaporation. This system can achieve faster growth rates while using less water than other hydroponic systems. When used appropriately, it can maintain the plants through flowering and ripening.

Deep Water Culture (DWC)

DWC is a type of hydroponic growing method where each plant's roots are growing in a tub of water. Plants sit in bubbler buckets above an aerated (typically chilled) water/nutrient reservoir with their roots submerged in the oxygenated nutrient solution which allows for continuous feeding. It is called the Deep Water Culture because the plant's roots will remain submerged in water all the time. An air pump will infuse the water with air so the plants will not drown. The Deep Water Culture system promotes faster growth because growing cannabis in soil, roots grown in DWC do not need to expend energy to search for nutrients that the plants need. The plants have an unlimited supply of oxygen because of added oxygen in the reservoir. Also, since the plant is spending less energy finding what it needs to grow, it channels that energy to growth. In addition, with proper guidance and a quality set-up, DWC takes less time to maintain than the average grow. It is important to check on the marijuana plants daily as it common for root rot to occur when the roots are consistently in water.

This can be avoided by changing out the reservoir weekly and adding beneficial bacteria to the reservoir. Additionally, keeping air and water under control are very important measures to take; air temperature should be 75-85°F when the lights are on and will drop by ten degrees when the lights are off. Water temperature should remain at a constant of 66-68°F at all times, any lower than this and the plants will not flower because they are too cold. Apart from this, checking the pH level of the water, always using an aerator, neat reservoirs are important measures to take.

Having too many plants in one reservoir can lead to white powdery mildew, hence growers should cultivate one plant per reservoir to allow the roots to spread out and give the leaves and buds more space. Also, it is important to allow the roots to dry so that they are not always submerged in oxygen and are oxygenated.

Before harvesting marijuana grown with DWC system, the plants should be flushed. This is done by draining the bubbler bucket reservoir and adding plain (pH) neutral water for 2-3 days before harvest, the plant will use all its existing nutrients contained in the stems, leaves and buds.

Drip system or Top Feed

Drip irrigation works by delivering water slowly to the planting medium or soil using an emitter installed at the end of the irrigation tubing. Nutrient-rich water is dripped slowly at regular intervals into the growing medium where the roots can absorb it. Small droppers are placed right next to the stem or roots in their containers within the medium. It is a very good method to save water because unused water drains back to the reservoir to be reused or to a waste reservoir to be discarded. It has a very low evaporation rate and is good for stealth grows because it is noiseless. However, a drip system has to be checked regularly due to significant changes in pH and nutrient strength levels. Perlite, Golden Wool, coconut fiber or rockwool cubes are all good growing media to use in drip systems. The setup can also be used to water organic crops, and is especially useful in greenhouse cultivation where there may be a large numbers of plants to irrigate.

Ebb and flow

This system is also known as 'flood and drain'. It uses a pump to bring water and nutrients from a reservoir into the where plants sit in pots on a grow tray. Nutrient-rich water is pumped into the grow tray where it is absorbed by the roots and medium at regular intervals. The pumping stops and water is allowed to drain back into the reservoir from which it was pumped. This process repeats itself at regular intervals to ensure that the plants are properly hydrated. Growers use a timer to operate the submerged pump which might be susceptible to pump failure, power outages and timer outages. The success of this system depends on the timing of the nutrient delivery. Too few nutrients could kill the roots while too much could deprive the roots of oxygen. It is best to use a heavy medium (like rockwool) for this system as the pots will sit in solution and might float or fall over.

Nutrients Film Technique (NTF)

Nutrients Film Technique is like a cross between Deep Water Culture and ebb and flow. The marijuana plants are planted within netpots with a medium like rockwool. Plants are suspended in net baskets or neoprene collars above a grow tray. Nutrient-rich water is continuously pumped from a reservoir into the grow tray and the drains from the opposite end of the grow tray back into the reservoir. This arrangement delivers a continuous flow of nutrient-rich water to the roots but it is very important to protect the exposed root from light. The plant roots grow in a covered tray irrigated by a shallow, slow-flowing nutrient solution, so good aeration of the nutrient/water solution is essential for fast healthy growth. Aerating the water in the reservoir using water circulation, air bubblers and water sprays that come in contact with air assure oxygenation.

This method is more suitable for experienced growers because it is quite difficult to operate. One major problem with this system is that the water solution could fail to leave the tube, stagnate in the channel and kill the plants. Also, it is recommended for plants with short life cycle since the roots could fill the pipes and block the flow of nutrient solution.

Wick System

A wick system has no moving parts and is the easiest to implement. A plant sits in a container above an aerated, nutrient-rich water reservoir and a rope or other absorbent material (like felt) is placed through the middle of the growth medium and into the reservoir. Through capillary action, the solution from the reservoir climbs the rope, providing the plant with as much or as little water and nutrients as it demands. No pump is required for this system. The wick system is self-regulating; the amount of water delivered depends on the amount lost through evaporation or transpiration. As long as the reservoir contains water, the plants are being watered. However, this method is better for smaller plants as large plants need a lot of water may use up the nutrient solution too fast.

Capillary Floor System (CFS)

Thick polyethylene sheeting is laid onto a level grow room floor, under HPS lighting, in long narrow strips between one and two yards across depending on the lighting. Capillary matting (the thickest available) is then laid over the polyethylene right up to the edge. These mattings are about a quarter inch (0.6 cm) thick and they are made from soft polyester covered with opaque polyethylene perforated with small holes. They have great wicking ability and are used in sub-irrigation systems. The capillary matting is now saturated with nutrient solution and then covered with thick, lightproof, reflective plastic sheeting.

Where the plastic cover meets the tray edge, it is sealed with duct tape to prevent evaporation. The plant roots will grow out into the matting, they just spread horizontally across the mat. The feeding with this system is easily automated using a sump pump and timer. The matting needs to be saturated but not swamped with nutrients and water. Capillary mats are effective in irrigating containers up to about ten inches (25 cm) high. They are simple to maintain and a very efficient method of using both nutrient and fertilizers.

HYDROPONIC NUTRIENTS

For a plant to thrive it needs several nutrients, this is exactly true for marijuana plants grown hydroponically. In a hydroponics system, plants get all the nutrients they need from the solution. Hydroponic plants require the same nutrients as the one grown in the soil. That means growers have to keep their nutrients solution well-stocked with all the necessary nutrients: like oxygen, potassium, nitrogen, phosphorus, magnesium and an even temperature ranging from 66-68°F. Additionally, there are secondary and micronutrients that help the plant develop but are not needed in huge quantities; boron, zinc, copper, sulfur, calcium. Hence, growers tend to use fertilizers that have all the required ingredients for both the vegetation and flowering periods and are compatible with use in a hydroponics system. Some nutrient mixes are specialized to be multi-functional: they provide food and other services to the plant like enhancing its ability to absorb nutrients and boosting its antioxidant system and ridding it of toxins built up during periods of stress.

A mix of different fertilizers or a self-mixed fertilizer that contains exactly what the plant needs to reach their optimum growth is best for hydroponics. Nitrogen-rich nutrient solutions are suitable for the vegetative stage while phosphorous-rich nutrients become more necessary for the flowering stage. After growers create a nutrient solution, it is important for them to meticulously check the concentration of the fertilizer regularly since the levels of nutrients have a tendency to fluctuate.

It is also essential for growers to take an accurate measurement of their nutrient solution to make sure that it is safe for plants' consumption. First, growers need to ensure they have the correct EC (electrical conductivity) and pH reading. The EC reading is how to tell how strong the solution is and how mineral-rich the water is. The more the minerals, the higher the EC rating will be. In general, a reading between 0.8-2.0 is appropriate for growing marijuana but it will a higher amount of nutrient as it grows older. However, the EC of the nutrient solution also varies based on its temperature since the speed of electron travel is measured, and that increases as the solution gets warmer.

Another measurement that can be used by growers is ppm (parts per million) which is a way of determining how nutrient-dense the solution is. The most efficient way to take a ppm is to multiply an EC reading by 500 or 700 depending on the scale being used. An EC reading of 2.0 would be either 1,000 ppm or 1,400 ppm (depending on the scale). The lower the ppm, the less nutrient-dense a solution is. Generally, growers should aim for the following densities based on the plant's growth phase; seedlings/early sprouts-100 to 250 ppm, early vegetative stage-300-400 ppm, full vegetative stage-450-700 ppm, early blooming stage-750-950 ppm, ripening stage-1,000-1,600 ppm. When the concentration of the solution is too high, the plants effectively lock out water/nutrient uptake. At a ppm of 2000, the osmotic pressure is strong, and plants' roots use more energy to extract water from the salty solution. As the level of nutrient salts increases, the chemicals start to fight each other for water, causing the roots to work harder. The more energy the plants use to extract water, the less they have for growth.

Also, the pH level has to be balanced between 5.5- 6 for the plants to absorb the nutrients. If the pH levels are not appropriate the plants will not absorb the nutrients and will suffer deficiencies. Nonetheless, it will be beneficial for the plants for the grower to change the nutrient solution out regularly to keep it as optimal as possible.

Nitrogen

Nitrogen is one of the most important nutrients for plants' growth. It builds the foundation for enzymes, amino acids, proteins and chlorophyll. Chlorophyll is responsible for photosynthesis and the green colour of the plants. It is an essential element of tissue; without it growth quickly stops. When marijuana plants are in their vegetative phase, the amount of nitrogen needed is dependent on the temperature of the grow room. The lower the temperature, the lesser the amount of nitrogen needed. Marijuana uses more nitrogen during the vegetative cycle (before flowering) than in later stages.

Phosphorus

Phosphorous is very instrumental in helping the plants to transform solar energy into chemical energy. Phosphorous aids in root and stem growth, influences the vigour of the plant and helps seedlings germinate. It is extremely essential in the reproductive stages and flowering of marijuana. It is very important for the maturation and the immune system of the plants. Phosphorus is also important for the creation of terpenes, oil waxes and plant sugars that give marijuana its flavour. Therefore, marijuana needs a lot of phosphorous during its flowering phase so if they do not get adequate or even abundant supplies, it results in lower yields.

Potassium

Potassium is very important for early plant growth, photosynthesis and protein synthesis as well as flower formation. It is also responsible for the movement of nutrients, sugars and water in plant tissues. In addition, potassium is vital for longevity and stand persistence of the plant. It is necessary for all activities having to do with water transportation, as well as all stages of growth; it is especially important in the development of buds. Potassium aids in creating sturdy and thick stems, disease resistance and water respiration.

Calcium

Calcium is an important part of the cell walls of the plants. The element provides the strength of the plant as well as the retention and transport of the other elements. It strengthens plant cell walls and therefore stems, stalks, and branches. Therefore, aiding in root growth—mostly the newer root hairs. It travels slowly and tends to concentrate in roots and older growth. It also enhances the uptake of K.

Magnesium

Magnesium is essential for photosynthesis as it is a component of chlorophyll in plants. Magnesium also activates many of the plants enzymes required for plant's growth. It helps to support healthy veins and maintains leaf production and structure.

Sulphur

Sulphur is very important for proper growth of the root and for seed production. It is very functional in a plant's metabolism and for the production of vitamins, enzymes and proteins. Sulphur is essential during vegetative growth and plays an important role in root growth, chlorophyll supply, and plant proteins.

SOIL

Soil is great growth, all- purpose medium especially for beginners. Most soil does not require much supplemental nutrition because it already contains and retains most nutrients. It is very forgiving and requires less precision when it comes to watering and feeding the plants. Hence, it assures growers of a good harvest, more so because it requires less watering and has a stable pH foundation. Watering and fertilizer application are easier with soil because it gives more room to correct mistakes. Soil also contains beneficial microbes and nutrients that keep plants healthy though nutrients issues might be harder to fix unlike in hydroponics. Also, it creates favourable conditions for pests, mold and mildew to spread.

Working with and watering the plants can be messy however the soil medium can grow plants that are up to two metres tall, offering a lot of yield in return. The mineral portion of soils is usually made up of three main elements: sand, silt and clay. Each of them injects beneficial properties to the mix and each is needed in order to create a soil that promotes optimum plant growth. Loamy soils are composed of all these three elements mixed with organic matter. Clay loams can either be silty or sandy but are a little heavy and in wet weather can become saturated. However, adding organic matter and sand to clay loams increases porosity, although this may be a strenuous task. Sandy soils quickly drain water and nutrients so they need to be irrigated often because they hold no water reserve.

Sufficient amounts of compost, coir, peat moss, leaf clippings and planting mix add texture and increase its water- and nutrient-holding abilities. Silty soils are composed of very small particles with a high surface-to-volume ratio that makes them chemically active. They hold nutrients in a buffer of charged particles, releasing them as roots draw them out using dilute acids. These soils hold water so well that heavy rains can result in anaerobic conditions, meaning the roots will be unable to get the oxygen they need. However, sand and compost help increase silty soil porosity. Most soils are not one type, they can be sandy-loamy, loamy-clay or any other combination of the three.

Sandy soils

Sand is formed from ground or weathered rocks, including limestone, quartz, granite and shale. Sandy soil is known for its coarseness, large granular size and low pH. Due to this, it dries up quickly and does not absorb moisture and nutrients well. However, it offers good drainage, high oxygen levels and is a good option for growing indoors. Some sandy soils are particularly fertile, however, because they contain significant amounts (up to 2%) of organic matter. This matter also helps the soil hold water. Sandy soils are rich in potassium (K), magnesium (Mg), and trace elements, but are often too low in phosphorous (P) and nitrogen (N). Nitrogen, the most soluble of the elements, is quickly leached from sandy soil. Sandy soils are improved by spreading layers of composted vegetative matter over the garden area. Nutrients gradually leach into the soil and the protective layer acts as a mulch to slow evaporation.

Silty soils

This soil type contains minerals such as quartz and fine organic particles. It is a medium-coarse soil type. Silty soils resemble a sort of mucky clay when wet and look like dark sand or brittle clods when dry. Silty soils have decent drainage and are quite easy to work on when wet. This type of soil is one of the best for cultivating marijuana seedlings because of the minerals and organic substances it contains. Growers using silty soils must be irrigate their gardens frequently. Usually, silty soils support very healthy and hearty plants because they contain an excellent supply of nitrogen.

Clay soils

Clay soil consists of the crystalline particles created through chemical reactions amongst mineral resources. It is heavy, drains poorly, not easy to work with and does not allow root optimum penetration. Despite this, clay is beneficial for soil as it usually include important nutrients like potassium, calcium, magnesium and iron that make the soil fertile. The success or failure of a plant in clay soil depends on how well the soil drains. A reddish-colored clay soil (sometimes referred to as "red dirt") indicates proper aeration and good drainage. Blue or gray clays mostly have insufficient aeration for growing marijuana; they must be tilled and amended in order to support healthy growth. The addition of perlite, sand, used planting mix, compost, gypsum, manure, and fresh clippings helps loosen and aerate clay soils.

Loam soils

Loam soils are a combination of sand, silt and clay usually in a 40/40/20 ratio. It has at least 20% organic compounds and a neutral pH. Loam soils have excellent drainage, water retention; high oxygen levels and is naturally fertile. These qualities make it one of the best soil types for cultivating marijuana. Loams range from easily worked fertile soils all the way to densely packed sod. Loams with a lot of organic matter produce excellent marijuana.

CHAPTER 4: THE MARIJUANA PLANT

Marijuana is a hardy plant that grows in both temperate and tropical conditions throughout the world and can thrive in diverse and sometimes challenging environments. It is a heliotrope, preferring direct sunlight and open spaces, and so grows poorly in shaded areas. The many uses of this multi-faceted plant have historically made it a valuable crop, and today there are collectively more breeding programs for marijuana than any other crop. There are three distinct varieties of cannabis that are grown for their Tetrahydrocannabinol or THC content: Cannabis sativa, Cannabis indica and Cannabis ruderalis. Within each of these varieties lie a great number of individual strains, each with a different cannabinoid profile and medicinal effect. THC is essentially the substance that provides the soothing, medicinal qualities that many people associate with cannabis. Cannabis plants produce psychoactive ingredients called cannabinoids. The main ingredient of the cannabinoids that gives the high effect is called - delta 9 THC. Cannabis plants also produce the - delta 8 THC.

This ingredient is in low levels but does contribute to the high. On the other hand, some plants do not produce any THC at all. These plants have been genetically altered to produce very low levels of THC and are mainly used by farmers in some countries who have permission to grow cannabis for hemp production only. THC is are unique to the cannabis species and is not found anywhere else. Plants grown for their THC content are commonly called marijuana. The THC drug is principally contained in multicellular structures on the surface of the flower heads and smaller leaves called stalked capitate trichome glands. These appear as tiny, translucent, mushroom-like structures that are visible through a magnifying glass. The heads of these structures contain oil that is secreted as a sticky resin and that contains high levels of THC. Male plants have low quantities of THC and are usually removed from the crop to avoid the pollination of the females. Once a female has been pollinated all her efforts go into seed production, which is not what marijuana growers want. By leaving the female unpollinated growers get thicker, more resinous buds whose weight is composed of flower material, not seeds. The Spanish word for seedless is "Sinsemilla," and this is what gives these harvests their name.

Female plants also produce resin glands. Some of these glands may have lots of resin but are not very potent while other plants may have little resin but are very potent. When a plant is grown in optimal conditions, it has lots of resin and is very potent. Resin glands are produced all over the female flowers and new leaves. They can be seen clearly with the use of a magnifying aid. These resin glands are correctly called Trichomes. It is within these glands that growers find the main concentration of produced cannabinoids and THC. When a plant is in full flowering phase, the resin gland can explode or break dropping resin down onto the leaves below. This can also give the leaves their shiny frosty potent look during flowering. Terpenes are also major components of marijuana resin, just as they make up the largest percentage of aromatic essential oils contained in most plants. The scent of most flowers, herbs and spices are composed of these oils.

Cannabis is cultivated for one or more of three useful products the nutritious seeds, the fibrous stalks, the resinous flowers. Cannabis fiber, produced from the stalks of the plant, is used to make tough cloth, paper, and rope. Though all cannabis plants are of the same species, the varieties typically cultivated for their seeds or fibers are known as hemp. The flower and the resin that coats them, is used therapeutically and recreationally. These varieties of marijuana differ in in many ways including growth characteristics such as: height, width, branching traits, flowering time to yield, potency, taste, type of high, aroma, leaf size and shape. However, growers choose to grow the different varieties based on several factors like for the quality of the high and the growing conditions. Each variety flourishes best under particular environmental conditions. Generally, potency is a factor of genetics. Some plants have the genetic potential of producing high-grade marijuana and others do not. As indica strains have more chlorophyll than sativa strains, they grow and mature faster. Also, cross-breeding indica and sativa or a combination of the two varieties creates a hybrid. The resulting hybrid strains will grow, mature and differ medically in relationship to the in relationship to the indica/sativa percentages in each phenotype contains. The benefit of hybridization is that the grower can create strains that are tailored to other growers and patients' needs.

Cannabis Sativa

Sativas originated from equatorial regions like Asia, Mexico and Africa where the growing season is hotter. However, they are now found throughout the world; potent varieties such as Colombian, Panamanian, Mexican, Nigerian, Congolese, Indian and Thai are found in equatorial and sub/equatorial zones. They typically bloom later than indicas and require a long time to mature because they originated in areas that have a long season. They are not generally used for outdoor cultivation in colder climates, although some hybrids can produce good yields in such conditions. They are a robust species that can grow both indoors and outdoors although it has been labeled an outdoor strain because of its size. Pure sativas grow really tall and can average anywhere between four to fifteen feet. They have a tall, leggy stature with spacious internodal length and a large sprawling root system. Sativas have pointy leaves with no markings or patterns and can have up to thirteen, long slender, pronounced jagged, spiky serrations. The colouration of sativa plants range from light to dark green leaves. Sativas have long, medium-thick buds when grown in full equatorial sun; under artificial light with inadequate intensity, or even under the temperate sun, the buds run, or are thinner, longer and do not fill out completely. Sativa leaves can either come from the female plants from which smokeable cola buds or male plants called hemp. Hemp plants produce more cannabinoids (CBD) than THC but are grown mostly for their fibre content.

Sativa contains large quantities of THC and is usually very potent. It produces a cerebral or head high and that is described in such terms as psychedelic, dreamy, spacey, and creative. Pure sativas can also induce paranoia and irregular heartbeat so it is rarely used as a medicinal choice. The buds usually smell sweet or tangy.

Cannabis Indica

Indicas developed in the further north in the shorter growing season in the Hindu Kush region of the Himalayan Foothills in countries like India, Afghanistan, Pakistan and Nepal where the weather is changeable and growing conditions can be harsh. They are relatively short (under five feet) and wide, with greener colors and round leaves that have marble-like patterns. Indica leaves typically grow shorter and wider than sativa and have a recurring olive green colour. They are very convenient for indoor growing because they will mature fast (six to eight weeks after flowering) and do not grow as

tall as sativas. The flowers are usually thick, dense with flavours and aroma ranging from "stinky," "skunky," or "pungent," Indica foliage is very green and in some strains, leaves around buds turn reddish to purple. Short, whitish pistils might turn a purplish-red colour. Indica plants were developed for resin content, which was removed from the flowers to make hashish. Heavily resin-laden indicas are often fungus and pest-resistant.

The best indicas have a relaxing "social high," which allow you to sense and feel the environment, without analyzing the experience. Indica also provides a heavy, body high that has a pain-numbing, sedative and relaxing effect on users. Its strong sedating and pain-numbing qualities are highly coveted by medical patients.

Cannabis Ruderalis

Ruderalis is a wild strain that originated from Russia and is often found growing naturally across Central and Eastern Europe. It is a small plant growing to about a foot in height.

The leaves of Ruderalis possess five to thirteen leaflets and are very similar to indicas except they are somewhat narrower. Ruderalis is low in THC but quite high in CBD, as such it is not used recreationally or desired by breeders and growers. Remarkarbly, ruderalis is an auto-flowering variety which means it automatically flowers at a certain stage of growth regardless of day length. Hence, it is used to cross-breed other varieties to produce fast maturing and automatically flowering strains. Ruderalis is also quite resistant to damage by insects or diseases.

SEEDS

Marijuana seeds are rich in oil and protein and are used as a food and animal feed, as well as a source of oil for fuel and skincare products. They are the means by which growers starting germinating marijuana and they are easily purchased off the internet. Definitely, the most effective (and least costly) way to get seeds is by receiving them from a friend or a fellow grower. Another option is to use a seed bank that can find be found online. Viable marijuana seeds are usually hard and dark coloured. Most mature seeds will have a dark brown color with swirling or marbling patterns.

Seeds that are a sort of a pale green colour are often not mature enough and were taken off the plant too early. Seeds are kept in a cool, dry place away from light and can remain viable for five years or longer. Fresh seeds will have a 90% germination rate but this dramatically reduces over time. After three to four years the germination rate will have dropped to about 20%. Dormant seeds need to be made up of an average of 20% water they need to be stored away from heat sources. However, the downside of seeds is that half might end up being male and the other half female plants. For reproduction, the flower of a female must be pollinated by a male plant, after which the female flower produces seeds. Once the seeds are mature, the female plants begin to die and the seeds are either dropped to the ground where they grow into new plants or they are harvested for sowing, processing into seed oil and food products. However, only unpollinated female plants produce the buds growers need. This type of high-potency marijuana is called "sinsemilla" meaning seedless. Some varieties of marijuana produce male parts alongside female flowers on the same plant especially if exposed to some environmental stressors. These plants are known as hermaphrodites and sometimes can self-pollinate to create seeds.

Except for clones, a marijuana plant starts off as a seed. Seeds carry genetic information from two parent plants that can manifest in various combination, some identical to the mother, some to the father and many presenting various traits from both. Generally, growers will plant many seeds of one strain and choose the best plant. Growing from seeds can produce a stronger plant with solid genetics.

Feminized Seeds

Feminized marijuana seeds are bred to only produce female plants that produce buds, so there is no need to remove males or bother pollination taking place. Feminized seeds are produced by causing monoecious or hermaphrodite condition in a female marijuana plant. The resulting seeds are hereby similar to the self-pollinated female parents, as only one set of genes is present. This is sometimes referred to as seed cloning and produces no male plant. However, it also means that they will carry a hermaphrodite chromosome. Feminized seeds are achieved by several methods; by spraying the plant with a solution of colloidal silver, a liquid containing tiny particles of silver, through rodelization, a method where a female plant pushed past maturity can pollinate another female plant, spraying seeds with gibberellic acid, a hormone that triggers germination.

Feminized seeds are produced from a genetic female plant that has been treated with hormones; inducing the female plant to produce male flowers. This pollen is used to pollinate female flowers and produces seeds that do not contain any male chromosomes. Feminized seeds on average produce a 0-20% hermaphrodite-to-female ratio whereas a standard seed's male-to-female ratio is 50%. Generally, feminized seeds can save growers both space and time and only require that you keep a careful eye out for any hermaphrodites.

Ways of Germinating Marijuana Seeds

Marijuana germination is the process of getting the seeds to sprout. This happens when a white tendril bud appears from the seedling. This first sprout is known as marijuana taproot and the rest of the plant's root will originate from this taproot. Marijuana seeds need a very stable environment and at times, patience to germinate. It is best to germinate seeds indoors first before transplanting outside.

Starter Cubes and Seedling Plug

One method of marijuana germination is to use specifically made starter cubes and Seedling Plugs. It is also one of the easiest methods. Growers simply place the seed in the cube or plug, add water as needed, and seedlings automatically get the optimal conditions for germination. Each cube or plug specifically has a hole designed for the seed. Growers just stick the seeds in and pinch the hole closed with their fingers.

Rapid Rooter Method

Rapid Rooter starter cubes are suitable for all growing methods including hydroponics, coco coir and soil. To get started with this method, pH balanced water is poured in a petri dish or container that can hold the rapid rooter plugs. The soaked marijuana seeds are then placed in the hole found on top of the plug. However some Rapid Rooter cubes are round on the bottom instead of being a cube which means they cannot stand on their own. So they are best suited to a hydroponic setup where it will be place directly in its final growing container. The Rapid Rooter tray is perfect for germinating seeds as the standard tray fits most humidity domes.

Rapid Rooter starter cubes

Rockwool cubes

These are mostly used by hydroponic growers since it can be safely used in a hydroponic setup, holds a lot of moisture and is resistant to mold. However, it has a high pH so it must be treated and adjusted before use. However, it can be difficult to separate the young plant from the rockwool and growers have to be gentle when doing that.

Rockwool Germination

Jiffy Pellets

Jiffy Pellets are used in a similar way to rockwool cubes. However, they are not suited for hydroponic setups where the roots are grown directly in water but Jiffy Pellets can be directly transferred into soil or coco coir. Before use, Jiffy Pellets need to be soaked in pH regulated warm water so the pellets can expand.

Jif

fy Pellets

Planting Directly in the Soil

Growers can plant their seedlings in the ground directly. This is beneficial to the growers because they do not have to worry about the plants being shocked during a transplant. This method is perfect for ensuring young seeds have minimal interference since the fragile roots are protected by the soil. It involves the mixing of some potting soil and compost. Soil used should have a pH of approximately 6. The seeds are placed like six inches deep into the mix, then covered with a layer of soil and watered.

The soil is kept moist (Not soaking wet) by sprinkling water over it once a day It can take about one to two weeks before the seedling sprout becomes visible.

Soaking seeds in water

Another method to germinate marijuana seeds is to soak them overnight in slightly warm water. This method is especially effective for seeds which are quite old or have extra hard shells. This method can help wake up older seeds. To germinate with water, growers fill a glass with room temperature tap water.

Most viable seeds start by floating then eventually sink to the bottom of the glass after a few hours of soaking. Then the white taproot breaks through the shell while still in the water. Older seeds tend to need longer to need longer to pierce through their shell. However, seeds should not be left to soak for too long (over 40 hours) as they can drown.

Paper Towel Method

Growers can also use a cheap paper towels to germinate their seedlings. They do this by wetting a paper towel and folding the seeds in it, then leaving it in a warm place. It is important to use paper towels that are non-porous so that seeds and their roots can lay on top without getting stuck to anything. Porous paper towels are not good for germination because the roots actually grow into them instead of laying on top.

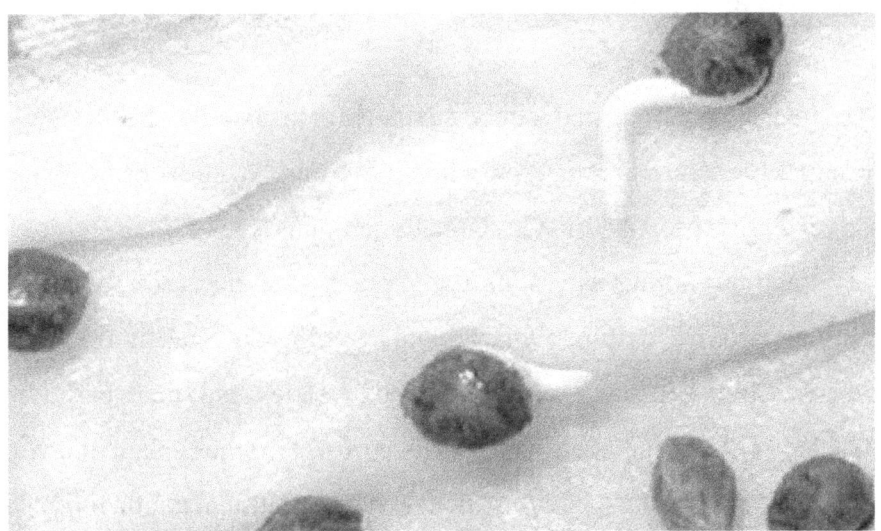

Paper towel germination

However, with this method lies the risk of hurting the taproot when moving the sprouted seed. This is because the sprout has to be transplanted to the soil or any moisture-locking media. The main root will be delicate so it should not be touched; only the cotyledon or body can be handled carefully. Also, the moisture in paper towel evaporates fairly quickly at room temperature so it is important that the grower keeps the seeds moist during the period they still need to germinate. The best way to do this is to drizzle some water in the lid of a petri dish, place open the paper towel in the lid the place the seed in the middle of the paper towel. Keeping the dish in a dark, warm place where the temperature ranges between 25-28°C is also important.

Cloning and Clones

Marijuana is propagated either sexually or asexually. Seeds are a product of sexual propagation while clones are a product of asexual or vegetative propagation. Technically, cloning is taking one cell of a plant and promoting its growth into a plant. Cloning is simply taking cuttings from a mature female plant. Cuttings are taken from the plants while they are in the vegetative state, and then carefully labeled. The cutting is basically a clone of its "mother" plant and will share the exact same genetic structure. These cuttings are then rooted and flowered. The resulting plant is a clone will be a 100% female crop. Therefore, there are no males or hermaphrodites to pick out from the garden with the buds.

Scissors or a sharp knife is perfect for taking cuttings.

Marijuana cloning should be done while the plant is in the vegetative stage. Plants that are in flower are difficult to clone so females are identified through the flowering of test cuttings. It is possible to induce cannabis to flower and then, as soon as the females are identified, place them back under 24 hours of continuous light, forcing them to revert to the vegetative cycle. However, this process can be time consuming and most growers prefer to use cuttings. Through cloning, growers can create a new harvest with the exact replica of their very best plants.

Seeds take several weeks to catch up to a rooted clone because cloning reduces the time it takes for a crop to mature. Most commercial growers use cloning methods to reduce the amount of time it takes for a crop to grow to maturity. Female marijuana plants can be cloned as soon as they have developed healthy side shoots. Once the female plant is healthy and mature one that shows signs of vigorous growth, a grower can make genetically identical copies of her that will exhibit exactly the same traits. A mother plant should be a vigorous, healthy female plant with plenty of shoots to take cuttings from.

When cutting clones from a mother plant, it is better to cut a large section of branch with multiple branches and bud sites. Bigger branches will support bigger buds. A sturdy clone will lead to a sturdy plant. It is important not to fertilize mother plants for a few days leading up to taking cuttings, this will allow the nitrogen content to remain little or nothing in the leaves. Excess of nitrogen in the leaves and stems will trick the clones into attempting to grow vegetation instead of diverting energy to rooting.

A clone

Growers need to work in a sterile environment and use clean equipments when taking cutting for clones. Start by cutting young growth tips, about three to four inches long, from the mother plant. Put the cutting in a small bucket of cold water so the stem can will absorb water while soaking; this prevents air bubbles from getting trapped in the stem. Use a sharp, sterilized pair of scissors or razor to cut the stem at a slight 45° angle to expose a larger area. This is to increase the surface area of the rooting surface, promoting faster growth. Then, dip the stalk into a rooting gel or hormone; gels have been proven to be better than rooting powders. Dipping the clone in gel first prevents the stem from getting clogged. Place the rooting gel you are working with in a separate container to avoid cross contamination of any possible infections. Remove any unnecessary, large leaves towards the bottom and clip off the tips of the remaining fan leaves; this aids photosynthesis, helping the plants to take up nutrients. Next, place the cutting stem ¾ to 1 inch into the chosen potting medium. The potting medium can range from a root cube to an auto-cloner.

When gardening organically, growers can use peat pellets that have been soaked in water overnight. An alternative is three inch pots filled with a good quality 'seed' potting compost. Simply firm the seed compost around the stem. Hydroponic gardeners can use rockwool starter cubes, floral foam or, alternatively, small pots can be filled with perlite or vermiculite. These hydroponic media can later be potted into soil for organic cultivation.

Whatever the potting medium used, growers should ensure that it is saturated before inserting the cuttings, but they should not allow the cuttings to stand in water. Excess liquid needs to be drained off as clone cuttings root more successfully in a well-drained medium and will not develop fungal infections. Place the clones in a high-sided propagator with a clear plastic lid and put it under a fluorescent or MH lamp on 18 to 24 hours of daylight.

Depending on the season, a greenhouse can be perfect for starting young clones and will not require any lamps. It is important to maintain humidity for the early stages of the clone's life, as they have no roots. Mist them three to four times daily for them to stay humid and alive. Cuttings are repotted as soon as they start to develop roots: usually 10 to 14 days after they have been taken. Once a cutting has developed roots it can be treated as a young plant.

There is an even less complex method of cloning using only water, light, and the cutting. The cutting is taken as with the other cloning methods; however, the clone is placed into a glass of water that has had foil wrapped around the outside to prevent too much light striking the root area. The clones are then placed under the chosen propagating lamp. They will even strike under a 100-watt incandescent light bulb in around 10 days Commercial growers prefer homogeneous gardens. Therefore, to assure uniformity, they usually use clones (rooted cuttings) from one plant or one variety so that the garden is genetically identical, or at least closely related. Using clones from the same plant allows commercial growers to maximize their crop, because the plants grow identically, thrive under the same conditions, mature at the same time, and provide predictable potency.

CHAPTER 5: MARIJUANA PLANT CARE

Transplanting

Some growers tend to sow their marijuana seeds in the same container they want to grow their plants in, bypassing the need to transplant their plants when they grow bigger. Indeed, this can save the grower some stress but small plants do not have an extensive enough root system to fill the container. Therefore, young plants can miss out on moisture and important nutrients and grow very slowly. When moisture remains in the container without being absorbed by the plant, it can lead to root rot which might damage the plant. Growing plants in appropriately sized pots and transplanting them as they get bigger is the best method for growing marijuana. The right time to transplant the plant is just before it outgrows its current container.

Marijuana plants that were germinated in small pots will need to be transplanted to larger pots as soon as vegetative growth starts to kick in. For plants to flourish, the root system need to stretch as much as possible and container size determines how extensive a root system can grow. If plants are grown in too-small containers, they can quickly become root-bound and start to lose vigor (or even die). Root-bound plants have a reddish appearance to their stems and will most likely have a nutrient deficiency. Repotting plants early helps them to form a healthy root ball in their new pots.

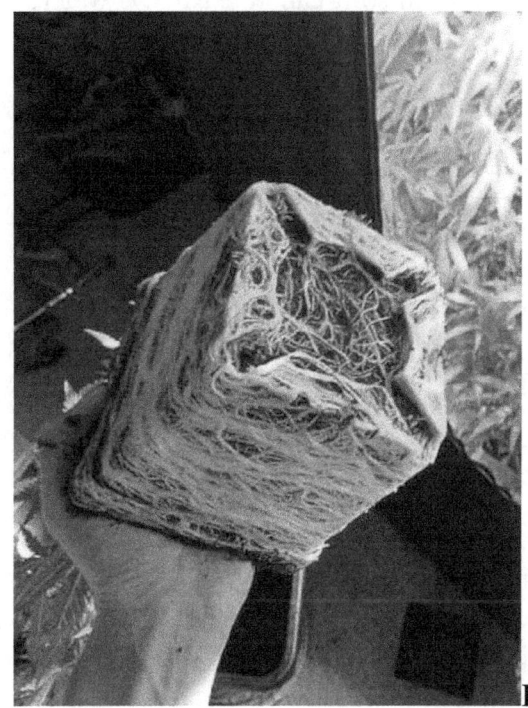

Root-bound marijuana plant

Root systems are very sensitive and damaging them could really harm the plant so the transplanting process should be treated with a lot of care and caution. When the roots are mishandled or agitated, they go into transplant shock. Plants should not be watered right before they are transplanted; refraining from watering allows the soil to hold together during the transplant process. However, the soil should be relatively moist so that nothing will be jarred out of place. Also, to avoid transplant shock, transplanting should not be done under intense lighting.

Growers need to make ready the new container with soil mixture. But it should not be filled to the brim so it can be easily be watered without the water running off the sides. The new potting mix need to be watered properly before the transplant, if this is not done, it might have a hard time absorbing water after the transplant. The grower can also add any fungus that benefits the roots like endomycorrihizae to the potting mix. Then, the grower turns the dry plant upside down and firmly pats the bottom. Next, grasp the plant stem from the base and ease the compacted medium out of the container in one piece.

Avoid grasping the plant directly by the stem. Grab the whole top and with a flat palm, and turn the container upside down because the plant might have to be gently pulled out of the container. Prior to this, a hole should have been prepared hole in the new soil. Place the rootball into the hole and cover it as best you can with the new soil. Then, moisten the soil immediately so that the transplant and the host soil can blend smoothly. If transplanting is done carefully and correctly, growers do not have to worry about the plants suffering from transplant shock and they will continue to grow normally.

Another method of transplanting is one that does not need the grower to remove the plant from the smaller pot at all. All the grower does is cut away the base of the small pot and place this pot into the bigger pot of soil. The roots will grow down through the bottom hole of the old pot and into the new one. The plant's roots will always find their way down.

Pruning

Growing marijuana in a spacious outdoor garden with plenty of warmth can yield a successful harvest, even without pruning or training it. In this case pruning is not required because the angle of sunlight that the outdoor plant receives is constantly moving. Therefore, the whole plant gets a decent amount of sunlight at some point during the day. This shows that plants will only try to find the best way to capture light by changing its shape and redirecting its leaves. Pruning creates open space in the middle of the plant allowing more air to flow through freely and letting light penetrate deeper.

However, the intent of pruning and training plants is almost always to increase yield. Many growers also use pruning to keep their crop trim and tidy. Pruning helps to keep the plant small while also optimizing it so that the best bud sites receive the best light. Pruning marijuana is merely the process of clipping pieces of the plant off. If the grower can remove these pieces in small and specific amounts, the result is a stronger marijuana plant. A certain amount of leaves will die off during the plant's life cycle and their quick extraction could keep the plant from wasting its resources on these dying limbs. By clipping these already dead limbs early, the plant's energy will be saved and more sunlight will reach the smaller leaves closer to the base of the plant. Besides, the plant will now grow faster and produce more chlorophyll because of a more efficient use of its resources. During pruning, low-down branches that receive little sunlight and bud sites that are low down and do not receive a lot of light are clipped off. By pruning, new branches, nodes and leaves are encouraged to develop.

As the marijuana plant grows and bushes out, it will start to take a definite shape and this gives the grower a definite sense of where the quality buds will grow so unnecessary portions can be pruned off. The process of pruning marijuana is delicate and could cause permanent damage to the plant. Pruning is best done in the second week of the growing phase well into the second week of the flowering period. Pruning should not be done after flowering starts because it can cause the plant to start producing vegetative growth again which will diminish the size and quality of the yield. Also, too much pruning can shock the plants and hinder growth because the plants will be spending a lot of energy to recover and not to strengthen bud-producing branches. To start pruning, clean and sharp scissors or clippers are needed to make clean snips while keeping the plants healthy and preventing infection/damage. The large branches should be removed first so space can be cleared for the more detailed work. Branches at the bottom of the plant should be pruned first as they do not receive enough sunlight and never become fully developed buds. Cut off the branches that are growing up to the middle of the plant, underneath the canopy. These branches will get shaded out and also will not develop full buds. It might take the plants awhile to heal from the pruning but in the days following a pruning the plants goes through an extra burst of growth because the open space will allowing the plant to get extra light.

Topping

Topping helps to maximize the plant's access to sunlight, typically done in an indoor grow room with limited light. It helps growers to make the most out of the relatively limited light source in the indoor environment. Topping marijuana plants involves cutting off the main shoot located on the central stem which stimulates the growth of more shoots and branches. By doing so, the grower encourages the plant to grow into a bush with a lot of shoots instead of one main shoot. Over time, it will turn the plant's overall shape into an upside down cone and the entire marijuana plant has access to more light. Simply remove the apical bud or the main stem with a clean cut or careful pinch between the fingers. Topping is particularly useful for growers whose growing rooms are not very tall as it encourages the crop to grow out instead of up.

The main reason a plant behaves like this when it is topped is because the centre of growth control is located in the apical meristem or main shoot. The main shoot sends suppressive hormones down to the lower or axillary shoots which stops them from growing rapidly. This is called apical dominance. The mechanism does not stop the lower branches from growing but as long as the main shoot is intact it will be largely favoured as the plant increases in height.

By removing the main shoot, the branches beneath it become free to grow at full rate in order to take its place. Also, when the top shoot is removed, the plant will no longer grow in that location, so secondary shoots make up the loss. Whereas a growing shoot might produce a larger individual cola, topping gives around four colas that can soak up the best light intensity. Moreover, topping marijuana plants diffuses hormones throughout the branches, encouraging them to grow more vigorously. Generally, topping leads to bigger buds, bushier plants with more branches and more leaves. Topping should be done the vegetative stage of marijuana plants. However, when marijuana plants are topped, they require recovery time of up to two weeks and this will prolong vegetative growth period. Also, topping is unsuitable for auto-flowering strains as they bloom too rapidly.

FIMing

FIM also known as the 'Fuck I Missed' method is a variant of the topping technique. By leaving a small portion of the growth on the main shoot intact, the plant will assume that four shoots instead of two are dominant and they will grow evenly in height. It also hardly slows down growth or reduce the height of the plant drastically. Simply remove 75% of the terminal bud or the tip of the main stem with either scissors or fingertips. A plant that has been fimmed is wider and has more leaves exposed to light, causing the plant to absorb more light. This will definitely translate to more yield.

The success of this method is uncertain but growers need to make they make the cut circular so that the remaining tissue forms a cup. Similar results can be achieved by topping the plants twice.

Lollipopping

By Lollipopping a plant during week three or four of its flowering stage, you give the plant lollipop look. The grower strips away the lower bud sites and leaves only the tops to fill out into fat nubs giving the plant a top-heavy structure. By focusing all the plant's energy into the top bud sites and not wasting any light on the leafy lower flowers, lollipopping improves the quality of the colas. This is because fewer leaves and fatter buds will develop.

**Lollipop**

ped marijuana plants

This method is particularly useful in grow rooms that have no side lighting to reach the lower regions of the plant. When the lower growth is removed, the plant will now have a long bare stem and one or more colas on top. Lollipopping should take place during the vegetative phase so plants have ample time to recover from the any stress before they start to flower.

Super Cropping

Super Cropping involves the crushing of the soft inner tissue of the stem. This technique allows growers to gain some control over the plant but it is mainly used to increase the health, potency and yield of marijuana plants. The soft inner tissue is made up of cellulose and forms a network of vascular tissue that can be divided into two groups namely the xylem and phloem. These tissues are responsible for the transport of water and nutrients along the stem. Breaking the plant's inner walls will cause the plant to rebuild it stronger than before and this why this method can increase the harvest. While rebuilding, the plant expands on the cellulose network which is why the stem grows thicker than before it was crushed. This allows for a greater transport of water and nutrients which will directly affect yield. Super Cropping can be carried out during the second or third week of vegetative growth. This technique can also be used when one bud is growing taller than the rest of the canopy. Position the branch by bending, tying down or gently snapping it.

Low Stress Training

Topping and Super Cropping can be referred to as High Stress Training (HST) which upsets the plant to a certain

Low Stress Training (LST)

An alternative to this is Low Stress Training (LST) in which the grower leaves the plant untopped but gently bends or ties down the main shoot at ground level instead. There are several ways to tie the top bud. The top of the stem near the growing tip is composed of flexible soft green tissue, so it can be gently bent down or sideways. To secure the stem and branches, use soft string or cloth, gardener's tape, twist-ties or stakes. The knots should be kept loose to minimize damage. The branch may have to be supported by splinting with a skewer or bamboo support. This has the same effect as topping because it is the main shoot that dictates how the plant will take shape. When the main shoot is tied down, all the shoots above it will grow more rapidly as the plant now assumes the main shoot is cut. With LST the main goal is to bend taller stems down and away from the middle of the plant so that takes on a flat and wide shape. The plant begins to grow bushier and denser and will produce multiple colas instead of just one. LST should be started in the plants' early vegetative stage and can continue into week two flowering. Both high and low stress training can be combined effectively.

Scrogging or Screen of Green (ScrOG)

ScrOG is quite ideal for an indoor grower that this growing few crops. ScrOG means that the grower suspends a net over the plants and allows them grow through it. This makes it easier to separate the growing branches so that they eventually cover the entire area of the grow room. The canopy of one plant can be grown as a large four-foot spread. The ScrOG net provides supports as the buds can often become heavy that the branches are unable to support them anymore and cave under the weight.

A Screen of Green (ScrOG) grow

Therefore, the ScrOG net removes the need for noisy fans used to make the stems stronger through the waving effect. ScrOG optimizes energy from the lighting by producing an even canopy space where bottom growth of the plant is forced upward to form a large canopy. Growers allow at least one square foot per flowering plant in the ScrOG method because the plants tend to grow very wide.

Sea of Green

This is a method where a multitude of small plants are grown instead of few large ones. These smaller plants will mature faster and in less time than larger and one crop can be started while another is maturing. Low stress training is needed here so the plants grow wide not tall. Trellis netting is laid above the plants to help them continue to grow wide. This method is mostly used by growers who want to use a small grow area. A SOG set-up can be any size but must maintain a certain overall shape. The final harvest result will be a full canopy of bud, hence the name Sea Of Green. Also, the lights should be kept closer to the crops since they are much shorter and smaller than normal grows. This saves growers a lot of time as less time is required between crops.

Sea Of Green

Regeneration

This is a technique used to harvest two or even three crops from marijuana plants by a process known as regeneration. Growers execute this technique by using mature plants, whose ripened buds have been harvested, to produce a second harvest. It can be used both indoors or out, but is most frequently used outdoors. It is done by carefully harvesting only the top third section of the female marijuana plants. Since marijuana grows and flowers based on the number of hours of light and darkness, manipulating its light cycle can convince a flowering plant to return to vegetative growth. The lower section is removed from the flowering area and placed into a vegetative growth cycle. It is better to leave the females under a continuous light source for the first ten days to speed up the reversion process, but they will revert under eighteen hours of daylight. When the buds are harvested, the growers leave undeveloped flowers and many of the leaves on the plant. Remove the buds from the ends of your plants' branches but leave all the fan leaves intact. It is important to leave as many of the smaller flowers on as possible, as these are the regeneration sites for new vegetative growth. The more flowers that are left on, the greater the potential for re-growth   Then they increase the light regimen to support vegetative growth; indoors leave the light on continuously; outdoors use night cycle interruption. Regenerated plants tend to have a lot more branching than first-time flowerers, so growers should practice pruning.

CHAPTER 6: PESTS, PREDATORS AND OTHER PROBLEMS

Pests are among the foremost and difficult problems that growers and gardeners face when cultivating marijuana plants. The best way to deal with pests is to make sure they do not enter in the first place. No matter the growing method, pests will infect the garden if they are given a chance. However, plants grown outdoors might turn out much worse than plants grown indoors when it comes to pests. While indoor growers might not have to worry a lot about pests, humidity here can rise to unacceptable levels, encouraging fungal infections and parasitic insect attacks. In the outdoor grows are protected by natural predators that help them keep bugs and insects in check. Spider mites, aphids, whiteflies, mealy bugs are few of the common pests that both indoor and outdoor growers have to deal with. Spider mites are by far the most damaging of insect pests and although they can be controlled with both insecticides and predator mites.

Marijuana plants are most susceptible to these pests when they are young and not well-developed. A single meal for a group of mites when the plant is a seedling could cause some irreparable damage to the plant and reduce it to nothing. Pests enter indoor gardens using pets as conveyance hence growers need to keep pets away from their garden. Their fur also accumulates on marijuana's sticky buds. Cleanliness is very important for indoor gardens so growers need to keep their growing areas clean at all times, remove any plant trimmings, and in larger gardens, use an industrial-grade vacuum cleaner that can suck up water spills. They can also wash surfaces and sterilize their garden equipments with a dilute solution of hydrogen peroxide. Indoor and outdoor growers should spray crops with a precautionary systemic fungicide every two weeks during flowering and humid conditions, using a treatment that contains carbendazime, a chemical that is recommended for fruit and vegetable treatment. However it is important to use the correct dosage and stop spraying at least ten days before harvest. Growers need to ensure that all vents in their grow room are filtered through stockings or pantyhose, since the fine mesh will trap flying insects. Any cracks, holes or other open spaces should be repaired.

Clothing worn outdoors can also carry in pests. Never enter your grow areas after working in outdoor gardens or walking through locations with other plants and foliage. Growers can remove their outer clothes and wear paper coveralls in their growing areas to avoid cross contamination. Additionally, always handle the plants with sanitized gloves and other devices.

Additionally, growers need to place any new plant in quarantine before letting the plant enter a pest-free garden, and use a pesticide/fungicide spray or dip just to be sure its pest-free. Marijuana cultivators also need to make sure their planting mix is composed of inert or pasteurized ingredients. Planting mix that is not inert or pasteurized may contain pests and diseases.

Spider mites

Spider mites are very common and are the most worrying pests in the cannabis garden. Mites are not true insects but arachnids; hence insecticides will not always work on them. They have four pairs of legs, no antennae and only a single body segment. Their colour ranges from red to brown, black, yellow and green. Colour exhibited depends on the food they are eating, species, and the time of year. Mites are very difficult to see without magnification since they are only 0.02 inch (0.4 mm) long. They live underneath the leaves but can also be found around the buds and spin webs that give growers a clue of their infestation. Spider mites multiply quickly and this rapid reproduction makes them a very worrisome pest.

These mites are deadly and can reduce the plant to nothing in two to three days. They feed on the chlorophyll of the leaves, leaving a speckled or mottled appearance on the leaves. Mites can greatly impact yield size, stunt plant growth and interfere with bud development. Spider mites are also vectors for disease, since they travel from plant to plant. As the population grows quite rapidly the mites produce webbing that they use as a pedestrian bridge between branches or plants. Spider mite infestations can be avoided by keeping the grow room sanitary. This includes using a fine dust filter in the ventilation system so all incoming air is cleaned properly. Growers should also keep sanitary soil and supplies, hands and clothing that will be used in the grow room. To get rid of mites, growers can begin by pruning the damaged parts of the plants, taking extra care to get rid of any webs created by the mites. After this is done, the plant should be cleaned off with a high powered hose containing water and alcohol with water constituting at least 60% of the mixture to avoid damaging the leaves. The plants should also be sprayed with insecticidal soap which weakens their shell and smothers many of the mites, lowering the population and the damage.

Spider mite on leaves

Neem oil is an organic pesticide often used to control mites but it has a foul smell that might affect the bud taste and leaves an oily residue that builds up with regular spraying. Pyrethrum is effective against some mite populations, but others have developed immunity to it. Natural predators like ladybugs can also be used kill off mites and other pests. Spider mites thrive in hot, dry climates. Relative humidity of 55-60%, average temperature of 25°C and a light breeze in the grow room slows spider mite development and reproduction.

Aphids

Aphids are small, fast-reproducing, pear-shaped, soft-bodied insects about one to ten millimeters long. There are thousands of species that vary in color from green to yellow, black or brown. Depending on the species and the stage of life the aphid is in, it may have wings, wax or "wool" made from webbing they secrete, or other unique features. A characteristic that distinguishes aphids from all other insects is the pair of tailpipe-like cornicles which extend from their abdomen. Aphids usually stay on marijuana leaves, stems and feed on the plants causing the leaves to wilt and curl as well as yellow till they die off completely. They puncture stems, branches and leaves and suck sap from them using a straw-like mouth, called a cornicle.

Signs of an aphid invasion include yellowing leaves, colonies and honeydew under stem and leaves. Another problem with this pest is that it secretes large amounts of honeydew, a sugary substance which is known to attract ants. To obtain enough protein, aphids suck a lot of juice, refine the protein and excrete the concentrated sugar solution referred to as "honeydew," which attracts ants that herd the aphids, protecting them from predators. Honeydew is a growth medium for sooty fungus, which causes necrosis of plant tissue. Sooty mold also discolours the plants, making them unsafe to smoke.

With their ability to fly from plant to plant, aphids are vectors for hundreds of diseases and can quickly cause an epidemic. They transfer viruses, bacteria and fungi from plant to plant. Aphids reproduce very fast and can destroy an indoor garden in not time so they need to be prevented or eradicated quickly. Outdoors, aphids are usually not much of a problem because of natural predators such as lady beetles, lacewings and syrphid fly larvae.

Aphids on marijuana buds

Ironically, over-fertilization can cause the appearance of aphids. Like other pests, aphids can be prevented by practicing basic sanitary measures like changing clothes before entering the cultivation area to avoid bringing in aphids from outside. Decaying leaves should be removed as soon as they are detected. Herbal oil pesticides containing essential oils distilled from plants that are effective and safe for people and pets but not pest can be used to spray already infested plants. Also, the aphid marijuana plant pests can be crushed or removed. For organic growers, introducing plant-friendly predators to feed on the aphids is another solution to an infestation. An application of a garlic oil mixture or a vinegar and water solution can also help to get rid of aphids.

Whiteflies

Whiteflies look like tiny moths and behave a bit like spider mites but are neither moths nor true flies. They are about one to two millimetres long and usually are a whitish colour. Their soft bodies are covered in a powdery wax which gives them protection and their white color. They are easy to detect because when the plant is disturbed they take flight and a mass of tiny white flies can be seen fluttering around the plant. They also leave a white waxy powder underneath the plant. Like mites, they stay underneath the leaves and suck sap out of the plants.

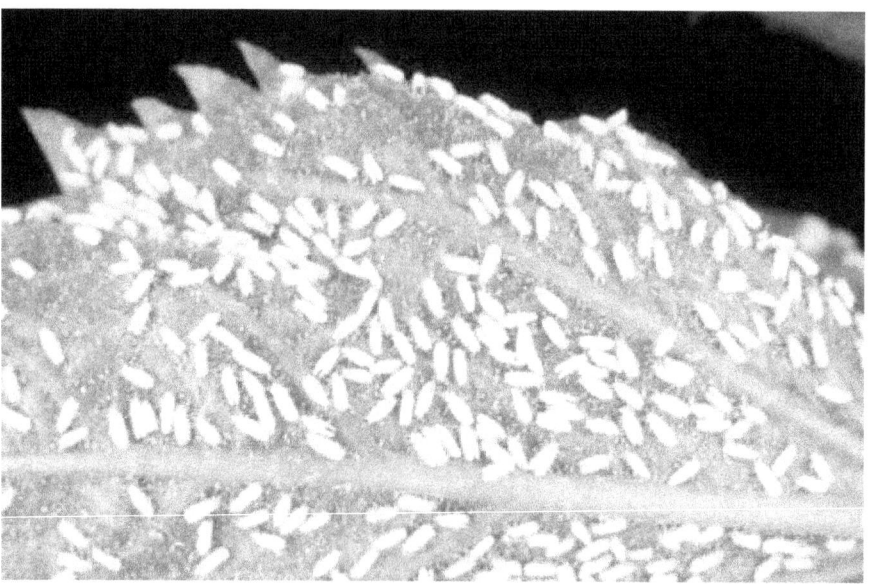

They feed on the nutrients of the leaves and leave mottled spots much like mite damage. Whiteflies are very fast at reproducing and females each lay about 100 tiny eggs on the undersides of leaves.

Eggs hatch in about seven to ten days, and the larvae drain sap from leaves. To prevent whiteflies, it is best to keep the temperature of the garden below 80°F (27°C) to slow whitefly reproduction, clear out plant debris quickly and install a fine dust filter in the vents to prevent whiteflies from entering through the vents. To get rid of whiteflies, growers can use strategically placed flycatchers - sticky strips of brightly colored plastic card that can be hung around the plants and are very effective at controlling aphids and whiteflies. They are attracted to the card and stick to the surface. The plants can also be sprayed with neem oil or potassium soap. Likewise, growers can shake plants to dislodge whiteflies and then suck them out of the air with the hose attachment of a vacuum cleaner.

Fungus Gnat

Fungus gnats also known as 'sciarid flies' are about two millimeter long, dark grayish black in color and have a slender build with delicate long legs and long wings. They prefer moist places and live at the base of the plants. Fungus gnats are a common problem for indoor growers especially those with poor watering habits. They are found outdoors occasionally in moist warm areas. Their larva grows in wet soil and they often appear when the topsoil stays wet too long between watering. The larva damage plants' root and reduce soil drainage, therefore weakening the plant and making it more susceptible to damage and infestation. Adult fungus gnats may not eat anything on the plant but they spread diseases such as pythium – a common cause of root rot.

Sticky fly catcher

To prevent a fungus gnat infestation, overwatering plants should be avoided because they thrive in wet conditions. Fungus grows in overwatered soil so gnats lay their eggs in the top layer of wet soil. Keep the topsoil as dry as possible. Light breeze provided by a fan can help dry out the topsoil faster and most importantly prevent the gnats from being able to lay their eggs. Also, the screen on windows and vent should be tightly filtered to keep them from entering the indoor grow room. Growers can place a barrier like cloth or cardboard over the soil so the gnats have no place to lay their eggs. Indoor growers can kill as much gnats as possible with sticky cards and also use it to keep track of how bad the infestation is; as the infestation reduces, there will be less adults caught in the sticky traps. Organic treatment such as neem oil, cinnamon oil, pyrethrum, Bacillus thuringiensis (beneficial bacteria) and diatomaceous earth can be used to battle a gnat infestation. Diatomaceous earth is an organic insect killer made of fossilized shells that puncture and desiccate small soft-bodied creatures such as fungus gnat larvae.

Thrips

Thrips are not commonly considered pests of marijuana. However, in some greenhouse conditions they can be serious pests. Thrips are tiny no more than 0.06 inch (1.5 mm) long but can still be seen by the naked eye. They are fast moving insects that are almost invisible to the naked eyes. Young thrips look like tiny, unmoving pale worms on leaves. Adults have wings but do not fly well; they jump when startled. Their presence can be marked by silver marks on the surface of the cannabis leaves, they also make the leaves brittle. Thrips use a saw-like structure to pierce and scrape the flesh until sap begins to flow.

Thrip damage

They then suck up the juices, and leave a surface of patchy white or silvery scrapes. The leaf surface looks scarred or scabby. Eventually the leaves look like all the chlorophyll has been drained, and they turn white. Thrips leave behind greenish black specks of poop on and under leaves. Thrip damage can resemble that of spider mites or leaf miners at first, but more severe cases result in the color-stripped leaves.

Damaged leaves cannot be healed and their ability to absorb light is compromised. If the thrips are not controlled the plants die. Thrips also carry pathogens that transfer diseases that are even worse than anything the thrips can cause. Outdoors, thrips hibernate over the winter in soil and plant debris. Thrips become active when the temperature climbs above 60°F (16 °C). The warm, stable temperatures of indoor gardens allow them to be active year-round. Thrips are a more serious problem indoors because of this, and also because a natural soil-dwelling fungus that infects thrip pupae is not present indoors. As with most pests the best way to deal with Thrips is trough preventative action by using high quality compost and maintaining a clean environment for the plant. Thrips are drawn to the colors blue and yellow, so it is best to avoid having yellow walls or items around your Cannabis gardens. Yellow and blue sticky cards can be used as indicator traps to detect an infestation of thrips. Spraying with garlic or neem oil and potassium soap could be useful to deter/repel thrips, unless the plant has started to flower.

Slugs/snails

Slugs/snails are a common pest for any outdoor marijuana grower, they are rare indoors. Slugs range in color from pale gray to tan, and grow to as long as 2 inches (5 cm) long. Their bodies are soft and fleshy, and glisten with a clear slime that the slugs secrete to retain moisture and help their movement. Snails are slugs with shells. They are built almost identically to slugs, except for a coiled shell of calcium carbonate that protects most of a snail's body. Snails can withdraw completely into their shells when threatened. Shells of common garden snails can reach up to 1.5 inch (3.75 cm) in diameter, and are colored gray, brown, and black. Snails and slugs are found on the leaves and edges of leaves and flowers and mostly attack plants at night. Spotting them is relatively easy since they leave a shiny trail of transparent mucus in their trail and the holes they create in leaves often have scalloped edges. Snails and slugs eat leaves. They leave holes in leaves and/or clipped edges of leaves and flowers. They especially attack young plants with leaves close to the ground because they like to eat tender cannabis leaves. They both feed on plant matter and will cause a lot of damage to the plants' leaves and buds.

Snails or slugs damage

A natural way to prevent slugs/snails is to create an environment that is conducive for amphibians like frog and toad as they are natural predators. This can be done by adding ponds and water features near the plant. Another way to prevent and kill snails and slugs is with iron phosphate, sometimes called ferric phosphate. It is completely effective and requires little effort. It comes as a powder or granules and is not harmful to plants, pets or humans. Growers can also remove snail and slugs manually at night when they are active. Also, growers can just apply salt to the garden area to make it inhospitable for the slugs. Alternative treatment includes building a barrier around the crop, placing baits and lures and using the predatory slug Ruminia decollate. A bait of jam and beer can also be used to lue snails to their death as they love the smell of beer and will basically drown in it.

Ants

Ants are problems for both indoor and outdoor growers. Ants can be found in the soil or planting medium, where they nest. They dig tunnels and nest in underground colonies causing damage to the roots and making it difficult for the plant to get good nutrient while also damaging water circulation in the roots. Ants are attracted to plants that already have aphids, whiteflies, mealy bugs, and scale. Then they take these pests to new grazing areas. First they spread out on the plant, then move the herd to new plants. Aphids, mealy bugs, and whiteflies secrete a sticky substance known as "honeydew," a sugar concentrate of the plant's sap. Ants eat it, but it also supports sooty mold. It is important to exterminate ants because they herd insects, and their nesting results in root damage.

Most of the species that affect marijuana use it for grazing their herds of aphids and mealy bugs. Ants are very bad for the cannabis plants because their presence usually heralds the presence of another pest usually an aphid or mealy bug infestation. They climb the stalk of the plant and graze their herds of aphids and mealy bugs on the leaves. When aphids feed on the plants, ants usually subsist on their honeydew for nutrients; therefore they protect the aphids, allowing their colonies to grow.

Cinnamon, cloves and bay leaves are known ant repellants especially for small gardens. It works as both a repellant and an exterminator since the ants are repulsed and killed by it. Also, the addition of cornmeal into the substrate also helps to get rid of ants. Ground diatomaceous earth is effective in killing insects with its sharp points, which puncture insects crawling over it. It is effective when it is dry, but not when wet. Growers can spray the plants with Pyrethrum. Pyrethrum is natural and harvested from chrysanthemum which is lethal to ants. Boric Acid baits can be used by growers as ants are attracted to either in greasy or sugary foods. Sweets and fats mixed with boric acid will get rid of any ant. Additionally, sticky cards, flypaper, or petroleum jelly are effective in making barriers and capturing ants. Beneficial bacteria like Saccharopolyspora spinosa that kills fire ants and some other species can be used by growers to control ants.

Leaf Miners

This is quite a selective pest because it does not affect all strains of marijuana. Leaf miners are not common in indoor marijuana gardens. Outdoors leaves are occasionally attacked by this pest and they remain a threat to the plant or yield. Leaf miners are usually the larval form of various fly species although a few species of moths and beetles also produce leaf-mining larvae. These larvae are very small maggots, seldom more than 1/10 inches (three millimetre) long and range in color from white to pale green. The adult leaf miner is about 1/12 in (two millimetre) long, closely resembles a housefly and lays its eggs under the plants leaves.

They plant their eggs deep inside the leaves and they keep multiplying. Just like the name sounds, its larvae dig tunnels and mine the top of marijuana plants. It damages the plants cells and drains out essential nutrients.

Leaf miner damage

White or brown lines can be seen along the top of leaves when the larvae are making their peculiar tunnels and eating any plant material in their path. Leaf miners leave the plants open to pathogens and fungi. Leaf damage causes low yields. When the females dig to lay eggs, plants secrete a sap that attracts ants and flies, thus inviting more infestations and problems.

Leaf Miners are not very likely to appear indoors but growers can follow the path of the larvae on the leaf and remove it with their nails. The leaves affected should be removed and discarded by growers. Naturally occurring parasitic wasps usually help control the population of leaf miners. In the outdoors, Herbal oil based pesticides and insecticides can be sprayed on the plant. Also, neem oil and other horticultural oil can be used to treat the plant. Pyrethrum and Spinosad are also useful treatment against leaf miners.

Caterpillars/worms/cabbage loopers

Caterpillars are common outdoors in spring and summer but quite rare indoors. Caterpillars are the larval stage of butterflies and moths. They have soft, segmented bodies with a head, thorax and abdomen.

The thorax contains three pairs of jointed legs that have hooks and the abdomen has five pairs of stumpy legs. Caterpillars are often the same color as the leaves so they are hard to spot. There are various types of caterpillars that usually infest cannabis plants. Cutworms are moth larvas that grow to 1 to 1.5 inches (2.5 to 3.75 cm) long. Colors include brown, green, gray and black. Cabbage loopers caterpillars are green, usually with narrow white stripes along the body, and may grow up to 1.5 inches (3.75 cm) long. Leaf-eaters are "wooly bear" caterpillars, their bodies are covered with long hairs that look much like fur. Corn borers are about 1 inch long, light brown in color with a brown head and spots on each segment. Some caterpillars eat leaves while others bore into the stem and eat the pith, the stem's soft inner tissue. Cutworms feed at night, and spend the day in shallow burrows near the plants.

They are cannabis pests that have a voracious appetite and feed on the plant at a very fast rate. They need to vegetate in order to form their chrysalis hence they can destroy crops in no time at all. They have a voracious appetite that will often go unnoticed until they have done significant damage to the plants. The borer variety of caterpillar will burrow into the plant's branch and eat it from inside out. If growers do not pay attention and it is a main branch, the plant might be dead and hollow before they realize there is a pest problem. Yellow or translucent eggs, small teeth marks and black droppings on leaf surface are all signs of a caterpillar infestation. Caterpillars bite out huge chunk from leaves and leave the leaves damaged beyond healing. Cabbage worms and other caterpillars also infest buds. In addition to the direct damage they cause, caterpillars leave behind damaged tissues that are vulnerable to infection.

One way to prevent a caterpillar infestation is to prevent butterflies and moths from hanging around the marijuana garden as they lay the eggs that hatch into caterpillars. Caterpillars on marijuana plants can be easily spotted and removed by hand. BT, Bacillus thuringiensis is a living bacterium that the caterpillars ingest. They sicken the caterpillars so they stop eating and die within a short time. When they die they release new generations of bacteria that are hungry for caterpillars as well. Growers can introduce Trichogramma wasps or spined soldier bugs to the plantation. They are several species of tiny stingless wasps that attack and destroy caterpillar eggs before they hatch. Alternative treatment includes applying garlic and pepper insecticide as they repel egg-laying moths.

Mealy Bugs

Mealybugs are named for the white, "mealy" wax that covers their bodies. On plants they look like tiny puffs of cotton, usually in crevices and joints between branches. Mealy Bugs thrive in warm temperatures and cannot tolerate the cold. Female mealybugs feed on plant sap and colonize the stem right at the soil level, where the stem joins the roots. A large number of mealy bugs can harm the marijuana plant. They spread even on harvested drying crops. An appearance of ants usually heralds a mealy bug infestation. They have developed a symbiotic relationship with ants, similar to that of aphids. Ants protect and herd them to collect the "honeydew," concentrated sugars that they exude as waste. If there are no ants to eat it, it is quickly colonized by sooty mold. The plant is weakened by the insects' sap sucking action on their vital juices and the honeydew droppings create mold infections on the stems and leaves. Mealy bugs are also often vectors for plant diseases.

A sign of mealy bugs infestation is the appearance of white, gauzy balls that the bugs weave, some of the leaves might also begin to develop blotchy patches. Mealy bugs can be picked or wiped off the plant by growers because the plant's structure does not offer easy places for them to hide and protect themselves. Natural products like lemon juice can be sprayed on the plant to deter this pest. Parasitoid wasps that are specific to various species of mealybugs and scale are available. Some wasp species include Leptomastix dactylopii, Anagyrus pseudcocci, and Metaphycus helvolus. Also, mealybug destroyer, Cryptolaemus montouzieri is a ladybug that preys on many species of mealybugs. Consistently treating the plants with insecticidal soaps and neem oil will see mealy bugs eradicated completely.

Pest Predators

Predators are insects that prey on the pest species that attack cannabis plants. These pests have no interest in attacking the marijuana being grown but they have an appetite pest and insect eggs. They are harmless to the crop, and their numbers, once released into the growing area, will be determined by the size of the pest problem. Once the predators have destroyed the pest species, they will die out. Friendly insects like ladybugs and assassin bugs are generalist predators that help to control pest population.

Ladybug

The ladybug is a brightly coloured beetle, usually red or yellow with round, black spots. They have an oval shape. A large part of the head and thorax are covered by the neck shield and its back end is covered by two wing cases. They are easy to find and are probably already living in the garden. Ladybugs have a great appetite for aphids, mites cochineal and small caterpillars; they are sometimes called aphid guzzlers. A ladybug is such is an aggressive predator that it can eat up to 500 aphids in a day and will consume over 5,000 aphids in its lifetime. However, the yellow variety of ladybug does not eat aphids but mildew so it is not much help to growers. In fact, it is a carrier and spreader of diseases.

Predator mites

The Phytoseiulus persimilis predator mite has a red-brown colour and is about the same size as a red spider mite. The diet of the predator mite consists solely of red spider mites. An adult predator mite feeds on spider mites at any stage of their life cycle including their larvae and eggs. In a day, an adult Phytoseiulus can consume around thirty spider mite egg or larvae, thirteen protonymphs or five adult spider mites. Due to its fast development and voracious appetite, the predator mite can fully eradicate a spider population. However, it is important to use the predator mite as early as possible after detecting the first spider mite colony give that mites multiply more quickly especially in the summer.

Predator mites

Amblyseius californicus is another mite that consumes spider mites. These species can withstand high temperatures making them good for growers in hot regions of the world.

Green Lacewings

The body of a lacewing has a greenish or yellow and is slender and long. They come in many species and sizes but the green lacewing is the more common than the brown one. Lacewings consume enormous quantities of aphids, especially when they are larvae. Lacewing larvae viciously attack all soft-bodied pests, including spider mites, and are particularly effective against aphids.

They kill even when they do not need to feed, leaving punctured victims to die of their wounds, and they will consume up to fifty aphids per day for three weeks before emerging as adults to repeat the cycle. Adult lacewings are nocturnal in nature and mainly feed on honeydew (secretions of aphids) and pollen. Lacewings also devour pests such as whiteflies, leafhoppers and mealy bugs. Growers can pull this beneficial insect into their garden by planting dill, angelica, golden marguerite and coriander.

Praying Mantis

The praying mantis is also a beneficial insect used for its stealth, patience and deadliness. They are primarily inhabit tropical and sub-tropical regions of the world. Mantises prey on invertebrates such as spiders, hornets and ants. They are generalist predators and appease their appetite with any insect they happen to come across. However, this means they can sometimes kill other beneficial species. Growers can pull this beneficial insect into their garden by planting any member of the rose or raspberry family.

Assassin Bugs

Assassin bugs are pest predators that feature specific adaptations that allow them to detect, stalk and dispatch prey. They have a long, piercing beak, long legs and round red eyes. The most commonly found type is brown-black with light flecks on cases of the wings. They are good predators that feed on aphids, leafhoppers, caterpillars and beetles. Assassin bugs stay perfectly still in place for their victims, puncture them and inject them with a deadly toxin. But the assassin bug is sensitive to various chemical plant protection agents; hence growers should be careful of the chemical they apply when they have this bug in their garden.

Birds

A number of birds including blue jays, robins, martins, chickadees and others are adept predators when it comes to killing off marijuana pests. To attract these birds, some growers can install bird houses, feeders, and pools of water. It is also favourable for growers to allow a few chickens, ducks, or geese run through the garden every once in a while as the plants grow larger. These birds will take out many pests along with a number of different weeds and growers will not have to do any work in that regard. However, birds can be a problem for growers that have just sown their seeds. Crows, sparrows, and starlings can be potentially harmful to your crop because they like to feed on the marijuana seeds. Other insect predators include frogs, toads, snakes, turtles, and lizards which all should be encouraged to take up residence in your garden.

<u>Companion Planting</u>

Companion planting involves cultivating beneficial plant species in close proximity to the marijuana crops. These plants work in numerous ways to protect the cannabis crop against insects and pests. In this system, growers strategically plant different crops, vegetables, fruits and herbs together so they can harness the synergy to improve plant health and yield. Even though THC is a natural repellent that deters a lot of pests, many common garden pests are still not dissuaded. Several companion plants serve as a deterrent to pests due to their potent, sometimes pungent aromas. Also, the conditions of the growing environment are improved by planting these beneficial plants. Companion planting falls under the scope of permaculture which aims to replicates natural ecosystems for application in modern agriculture.

Basil strong scent has been proven to repel thrips, aphids, beetles, moths and whiteflies. It could also increase the oil production and flavour of nearby plants. Likewise, the pungent odour of lemon balm is capable of repelling gnats and mosquitoes. Dill and coriander can also be used as companion plants to prevent the invasion of spider mites, aphids, worms and potato beetles. The mustard plant fights nematodes and also acts as a natural bio-fumigate. Using beans as a companion plant is very beneficial because it helps to pull nitrogen out of the air and transforms it to nitrogen to be used by the marijuana plants. Borage plant is also useful for cannabis because it pumps additional vitamins and minerals into the soil. Companion plants also help to attract beneficial insects that can boost the health of the marijuana garden. Lavender emits a strong odour that attracts insects who will feed on the larvae of pest species. Chamomile plant also attracts honey bees and hoverflies while repelling mosquitoes and flies. Some organic growers plant garlic in with the crop. It takes up very little space, repels most pests and acts as a natural fungicide to protect against diseases. If you want to try this companion planting, buy a variety of garlic that has been bred for cultivation, as it will be disease and virus free. Do not use garlic bulbs from the supermarket. Chili pepper will deter large pests like deer, rabbits and rats. The root system of the pepper plant also exudes a chemical that protects against rot which is especially beneficial in areas with poor drainage or excess rainfall. Sunflower attracts beneficial mites and bugs which feed on pests of the marijuana crop. Its roots are helpful in soil filtration and preservation.

Several companion plants can also help to mask the sweet and skunky smell of the marijuana plants. Mint is a plant with a strong odour that repels garden pests and helps mask the smell of marijuana. Flowers and herbs like lavender, jasmine, rosemary and thyme that emit highly aromatic smell are especially great to plant near marijuana due to their overpowering scents. For outdoor growers, southernwood, a perennial herb that grows as tall as five feet is perfect. Apart from the keeping the garden obscured from prying eyes, it has a strong lemon scent that masks the smell of the cannabis grows.

Companion plants can also be harvested as medicinal teas and food while keeping the biodiversity high and soil healthy. This is because they improve soil conditions through aeration and nutrient promotion while sometimes providing structural support.

CHAPTER 7 : HARVESTING

Harvesting is the reward marijuana growers reap for their hard work, commitment and care of the plant. However, marijuana has to be harvested at the exact right time, not too early and not too late. Harvesting the crops at the precise time will allow for maximum bud growth and optimal THC potency. Harvest too late and the THC will begin to break down into CBD and lose potency, too early and the yield and buds are not optimal enough. Growers can determine the right time to harvest by either looking at the trichomes or checking the pistils. The trichome method is considered the most accurate to determine the right harvest time. Trichomes are resin glands that grow on marijuana buds and are responsible for the stickiness of weed. Trichomes house THC and many other chemicals in the marijuana plant, so when growers harvest based on trichomes, they are trying to determine when the THC is at the highest level. When plants are ready to be harvested, the trichomes appear a milky, cloudy white under a magnifier.

If the buds are allowed to continue to mature, the white trichomes begin to turn amber. The more the number of amber trichomes, the more CBD and CBD elements in the plant.

Observing the pistils is the easiest but not the most accurate method for deciding when to harvest. Growers should check the buds' pistils to see what their colouring is, mostly white pistils means the plant is still too early to harvest look like. When most of the pistils (about 70 – 90%) turn brown or red, the plant is just perfect for harvest. Another sign that the marijuana plant is ready for harvest is that the fan leaves start turning yellow and falling off. Other ways to know the plant is ready for harvest is when the plant stops producing resin, smell has reached a peak and bud mass has not increased in the few days.

Orange pistils

Indoor crops are harvested within 45 to 75 days, depending on the variety and cultivation method. Most indoor marijuana is Sinsemilla, or seedless, since fertilized buds are less potent and their weight is composed mostly of seeds. When grown indoors, most marijuana strains will be ready to harvest seven to twelve weeks after the start of their flowering cycle. Most indica strains are ready to harvest within seven to nine weeks while sativa strains can take ten to twelve weeks to reach maturity. Auto-flowering strains are mostly ready for harvest in ten to eleven weeks. Marijuana growers need to be discreet when harvesting because the process will spread that potent marijuana odour into the air.

The marijuana plant can be harvested in a number of ways. The methods fall into two main categories: harvesting the entire plant or harvesting individual buds as they ripen. The advantage of harvesting individual buds as they ripen is that it gives the lower buds and buds hidden inside the canopy the chance to fully mature. This usually occurs within ten days. There is a significant difference in potency and quality between a slightly unripe and ripe bud, so the extra time and labour that multiple harvesting sessions or daily bud inspections entail are well worth the effort, even for large harvests.

Close-up of cutting

Another advantage of partial harvests, particularly for large crops, is that there is more time to process the material. A large harvest cut over two weeks is a lot easier to process than one that is cut all at once. However, this method is quite taxing for growers, especially guerilla farmers. To actually harvest the plants, all growers have to do is gently pull them up out of the soil. To facilitate this process, you might want to wet the soil beforehand. Growers or their helps should avoid bending or cracking the plants as they pull them up as it makes them harder to deal with. If the plants are in pots, then growers can simply pull them out or even dump the pot and all the soil out. Another method of harvesting the plant is chopping/cutting it at the base of the stem with a sharp, clean knife, scissors or hacksaw. The harvest process involves quite a few steps before the buds can finally be fit for ingestion.

Fan Leaf Removal

Once a grower has deemed his or her marijuana plant ready for harvest, the first action to take is to remove the large fan leaves. Their removal of fan leaves makes it easier for the plant to be hung dry by the grower; it also creates better airflow around the flower. It is the bulkiest material of the plant and with it out of the way, it is much eaiser to proceed with trimming. These leaves can be plucked by gloved hands, cut with scissors or removed with a device such as a handheld hedge trimmer.

The fan leaves are trimmed off because they do not contain a great amount of cannabinoids like the leaves closer to the flowers or the flowers themselves. Due to this, many growers simply get rid of them. Once the fan leaves are trimmed off, the grower can either trim the remaining leaves while the plant is wet (wet trimming) or begin the drying process and remove the remaining leaves after the plant is wet. It is at this stage that the grower labels the varieties or strains (if needed) to prevent it from being grouped with other strains in the drying room.

Manicuring

Manicuring is removing the buds and the rest of the leaf material from the branch. Simply put, manicuring is cutting off the leaves that were growing from the buds so that just the bud remains. The purpose of this is to remove as much of the leaf material as possible, thus exposing the flower. The loose trichomes that are broken off while manicuring are known as kief. Growers manicure their plants for several reasons including aesthetics, THC concentration and appearance. People associate manicured weed with good weed so untrimmed weed may look less appealing to them.

Hand manicuring

Also, leaves are harsher on the lungs when smoking so trimming off extra leaf matter improves the smoothness of the smoke. Manicuring should be done immediately after harvest when plant leaves are still soft and supple so the trichomes can remain intact. A good period to manicure is when the plants are nearly dry, when they are too dry, many of the glands will fall off with handling. Growers sometimes manicure a bit while the plants are still standing. The plants are in a convenient position to remove fan leaves and other vegetation so there is less damage to the bud.

Drying

Drying the marijuana plant is either done after the wet trim method or right after removing the fan leaves in the dry trim method. The dry room should be dark, well-ventilated with proper and gentle airflow. This can be achieved with floor or wall-mounted fans and adequate ventilation. The room's temperature and humidity should also be well-regulated preferably using humidifiers and dehumidifiers. The plants should be kept at 45-55% humidity with temperatures around 60-70°F. The humidity can then be lowered to 43-48% after about a week at the same temperature. Monitoring the humidity and temperature is very important as they have a direct impact on the quality of the marijuana. It is crucial to preserving the flavour and aroma of the harvested bud. Also, exposing drying buds to any light will rapidly degrade the THC content. Secondly, growers are less likely to have fungal attacks since you can ensure that your drying room has good air circulation around the drying crop.

Plants are placed on hooks and hung to dry from chain links or wires that are attached securely to the walls. Some growers cut and hang the whole plant while others snip the buds from the branches and then hang them to dry.

Buds hanging to dry

During the drying process, 75% of the water content will evaporate into stem and gas. The drying plants should be monitored daily to detect any fungal growth early. Fast drying techniques include using the oven, microwaving, and even using a skillet. Most growers are usually in a hurry to test out their plants and even though these fast methods might produce a harsher taste overall, they will still give growers the ability to smoke some bud soon after harvesting. Any infected flower should be removed from the grow room and disposed off properly. When the flowers feel a tad crispy and the plant's stem is no longer rubbery and does not completely break when it is bent, the plant is dry. Drying can take anywhere from seven to fourteen days before plants are ready for curing. If you dry too fast, the buds will take longer to cure while if you dry too slowly, the plant will be exposed to more air which can reduce potency.

Curing

Curing begins after the flowers are dry enough to cut from the stem. It is also known as deboning. While cutting off the flowers, a small portion of the stem should be left attached to the bud so it does not fall apart. Curing is done to improve the quality of the flowers. A good curing process involves correctly handling three parameters; temperature, humidity and light as these greatly affect the quality of the final product. Many of the terpenes that give marijuana its signature smell and flavour are quite volatile and evaporate at temperatures as low as 70°F. A slow cure at low temperatures will preserve these terpenes better than a quick, hot cannabis drying process.

Buds continue to cure when they are kept at about 60-70° F (15-21° C) with a humidity of 50%. These conditions also provide an optimal environment for enzymes and aerobic bacteria to break down leftover minerals and the undesirable sugar produced by the decomposition of chlorophyll during the drying process. As chlorophyll is metabolized, the bud turns a lighter shade of green. Other pigments, formerly hidden by the chlorophyll, become apparent, coloring the bud with red, yellow, and purple highlights. The presence of the sugars and minerals can cause the harsh, throat-burning sensation when smoking improperly cured cannabis.

For the curing process, growers can place the trimmed buds into an airtight container; wide mouth quart-sized containers are the most commonly used. However, ceramic, metal, wood or plastic can be used too. But most plastic bags are not can impervious to oxygen and can degrade when they come in contact with certain terpenes present in cannabis. The flowers should be packed loosely into the containers, filling it all the way to the top without crushing or compressing the buds. The sealed container should be placed stashed in a cool, dry place to finish the curing process. During the first week of curing, growers should open the containers several times a day to allow the buds breath. This also allows moisture to escape and replenishes the oxygen in the container. After the first week, the container can be opened less frequently. Depending on the strain, marijuana should be cured enough within four to eight weeks, some varieties benefit from six months or more of curing. After curing, the flowers should be at their peak flavour. Properly cured marijuana can be stored for long period without losing its cannabinoid content or growing mold. Well-cured flowers can be stored in a cool, dark place for up two years without losing its potency, flavours or odour.

Flushing

Right before harvesting, marijuana plants should be fed only plain water with no nutrients or fertilizer. This is called flushing. This is done to remove any fertilizer chemical that has built up in the plant itself and the medium it is being grown in. Failure to flush the plants, the resulting marijuana buds will have a bad taste and be quite hard to ignite. With hydroponic grows, the plants need to be flushed about seven days before harvest. This is done by switching from nutrient solution to distilled water that contains no nutrients. However, if the plant is being grown organically, there is hardly a need to flush because it has not been taking in any chemical nutrients.

CHAPTER 8: SECURITY

Starting the marijuana business involves a lot of intricacies concerning both legalities and location. It can be a much harder process than growers or processors initially anticipate. Even as legalization is continuing its advance across the world, each state has its own regulations and restrictions regarding zoning, growing, product standards, processing and security. There are a lot of security implications to be considered when growing outdoors or indoors. Cannabis is illegal in a lot of places and law enforcement agencies, bandits, and herbaceous mammals alike will target your plants. Even in most places, growing marijuana is a legal gray area. When choosing the location to site your marijuana grow house, safety features must always be foremost in your mind – whether pre-existing or new building. Growers can also get a marijuana growers' insurance to protect assets in the event of loss. Having and maintaining operational and compliant security systems and appropriately secure storage systems for their gardens is very important for growers. Indoor and outdoor security measures needed typically include video surveillance systems, alarm and notifications system, network systems and security personnel. Guard dogs can also go a long way in security. Many professional growers have dogs set up around the perimeter of their garden to guard against thieves. Whether it is a legal medicinal or recreational operation, the need for security cannot be overemphasized because of the desirable nature of marijuana and the easy street resale value.

Also, growers need to learn to be very secretive about their growing location. Whatever the location and requirements, the location of your grow room must be secret. In other words, do not show anyone or talk to anyone about the garden. Although it's natural for any gardener to want to tell everyone about their exploits, it is dangerous when the plant their gardening happens to be illegal. The most important and effective security measure any marijuana can implement is to never tell anyone about your garden. In most cases, a cannabis theft is carried out by a friend or confidante. Hence, background checks and serious evaluation of the character of the people you recruit to help you with keeping your grow safe.

Camoufl aged plant

Growers cultivating in hostile locations need to be able to disguise their garden by making it appear normal to public eye. Glowing lights or strong odours is a surefire way to be discovered by neighbours. Always make sure your lights are contained and odours are treated with a carbon filter or other odour neutralizing devices. Vents can be a concern, so try to position your ventilation ducts so that they do not allow odours to be detected. Place filters over the vents to prevent any pungent smells from escaping. Ionizers have some effect on controlling odors in smaller setups, and work by emitting negative ions into the grow area. Air purifiers that combine powerful ion emissions with multistage, odour absorbing carbon filters can be purchased and are ideal for smaller grow rooms. Odor absorbing gels that are made from essential oils and other plant derived compounds also mask odours.

To avoid suspicions of the grow lights, growers can use a blackout curtain that you can be left pulled down for most of the time spent growing marijuana. A blackout curtain will also help make the flowering period easier because it ensures that no outside light will leak in. Fans, exhaust fans, air and water pumps also make a lot of sounds, so it is important for growers to be careful about the placement of these equipment. Likewise, there are security implications to consider when purchasing seeds online, so never have seeds sent to your home address. Keeping your garden neat and arranged is also very crucial to outdoor growers. A garden that is littered with trash— discarded grow supplies, empty fertilizer boxes, broken pipe fittings, and other junk—irritates the neighbors and invites investigation and suspicion. Keep your yard clean and trimmed; keep your grounds and property safe.

It is also advisable to keep a garden to practice companion planting by growing vegetables and flowers that thrive in your region. Being a bad neighbour is a also most likely to get you in trouble, at the slightest suspicion that you are growing, your neighbour will likely make a report.

Guerilla garden planted on public properties is at the risk of being discovered by just anyone, so it is important for you to locate your garden away from any trails. You can camouflage your plants by having them planted amongst lush foliage and further using pruning, bending and training methods. Guerilla growers must avoid creating a track when they visit their grow area. Try to access your growing area through several different routes if you can. Even by visiting the same spot once every two weeks you will leave a trail that some hikers might see and use. Also, when growing on a large scale outdoors avoid leaving fingerprints in the garden or on any equipment, always wear gloves. Although most people grow indoors to avoid any security issues, there are still some problems that can crop up if they are not careful. In many jurisdictions, growing marijuana is still definitely illegal, and, if anybody suspects you, they might make a report. Apart from this another problem with indoor growing is fires. Some indoor growers tend to use very shoddy lights with even shoddier electrical fixtures and these results in major fires.

CPSIA information can be obtained
at www.ICGtesting.com
Printed in the USA
LVHW082100031220
673319LV00016B/1438